Teaching Preschoolers:
First Steps Toward Faith

Thomas Sanders
Mary Ann Bradberry

LifeWay Press®
Nashville, Tennessee

Item 005283656
ISBN 1415869219

Dewey Decimal Classification Number: 268.432
Subject Headings: SUNDAY SCHOOLS—PRESCHOOL/CHILDREN
                  CHRISTIAN EDUCATION
                  BIBLE—STUDY AND TEACHING

Printed in the United States of America

Kids Ministry Publishing
LifeWay, MSN 172
One LifeWay Plaza
Nashville, Tennessee, 37234

Table of Contents

Thomas Sanders is the Provost and Vice President for Academic Affairs at East Texas Baptist University. Dr. Sanders teaches preschoolers and children with special needs and speaks nationally and internationally related to children and their families. He also is involved in research with children related to their understanding of the language of faith and conversion.

Mary Ann Bradberry lives in Austin, Texas, is the Executive Director of the Texas Baptist Weekday Association, leads conferences on children's brain development, serves as an adjunct professor for Dallas Baptist University, and volunteers as a children's grief group facilitator at My Healing Place. Mary Ann and her husband attend Sunset Canyon Baptist Church in Austin, Texas.

Special appreciation to Cindy Lumpkin, Melinda Mahand, and R. Scott Wiley for their work on this book.

Acknowledgments to Sue Raley, Gayle Lintz, Ann Parnell, Rhonda Reeves, and Joanne Moran.

Special thanks to Melinda Mahand and Clara Mae Van Brink for their previous work on *Love, Laughter, and Learning* and for the groundwork in *How to Guide Preschoolers*.

Taking the First Steps Toward Faith

One day in Vacation Bible School, I had the opportunity to tell my favorite Bible story—"The Four Friends Who Helped." Do you remember that story? A man who couldn't walk had four friends who literally carried him to see Jesus. Yet, when they arrived at the house where Jesus was, so many people were already there that they could not get anywhere near Him. Refusing to give up, the friends carried the man to the rooftop. Then they started digging a hole in the roof so that they could lower the man through it and lay him at Jesus' feet.

As I dramatically told the details to my five-year-olds, they all seemed very interested and amused, except for one child. Nick seemed a little perplexed as I reached the end of the story. Finally, he blurted out, "Who fixed the roof?" Frankly, I could not answer his question because I had never considered this dilemma. I told Nick that I would let him know if I figured it out.

Several months later, I realized a deeper meaning to Nick's question, "Who fixed the roof?" A lifetime of hearing and reading this story had never caused me to consider Nick's question or the cost of the miracle—not just the cost paid by Christ, but by the individuals involved in the miracle. The four friends had brought their sick friend to Jesus, but an unnamed homeowner paid the price for the roof that was destroyed in the process. The friends also were not mentioned by name, but they were instrumental in the man's life. They paved the way for a life-changing encounter with Christ by physically carrying the man, overcoming barriers, looking for creative methods, and enduring hardships. Yet, the four friends could not perform the miracle; they could only prepare their friend by taking him to Jesus.

This story holds a great deal of truth for those of us who teach and care for preschoolers. As teachers, we take the role of the four friends. We pave the way for preschoolers by guiding them to take their first steps toward faith. These steps eventually lead to a decision later in life—for Christian salvation! However, these first steps toward faith, conversion, and spiritual transformation are not random, haphazard, inexpensive, or effortless. Building a foundation for faith involves a commitment by parents as well as teachers. A foundation is the most important part of a structure. It supports and undergirds everything within the structure. In the same way, foundational teaching supports and undergirds a child's life. Patterns developed early in life become the habits and basis for decision making in the future.

The 21st century has and will afforded Southern Baptists more opportunities for foundational Bible teaching in the lives of young children than any other denomination. Today, even with advances in research and a new understanding of the importance of the first five years of life, some churches, church leaders, parents, and even teachers have yet to catch the vision of what could happen if church and home "connected" in the ministry of laying spiritual foundations for life.

Coupling knowledge of preschoolers with the help of the Holy Spirit and power of the Holy Scriptures, Southern Baptists have great potential for changing the world for preschoolers and their families. Through Sunday School, children's choir, Discipleship Training, Mission Friends, church weekday education, Vacation Bible School, and other ministries, churches have indescribable opportunities to shape the lives of young children for God's kingdom. Major advances have been made through the strong commitment to teach preschoolers for Christ, but the goal has not been attained.

Dispelling Myths and Half-truths

Several myths and half-truths have limited most churches from having the most effective foundational teaching ministry to preschoolers.

Half-truth   **Preschoolers are the church of the future.**

Young children are our future, but they also are part of the church today. Focusing on future involvement of children often leads to a limited view of how young children can participate in the church now. It also limits the resources and leadership that may be devoted to teaching preschoolers. Churches frequently delay investing time, personnel, and resources in preschoolers until they are youth or even young adults. Valuable time is lost by this age in life—time or opportunity that will never be regained.

Half-truth   **Preschoolers cannot contribute.**

Young children do not have large amounts of money or a great amount of leadership to contribute to the church. Yet to say that they do not contribute is absolutely incorrect. According to Scripture, God focuses on the sacrifice, intent, and attitude of the giver, not on the size of the gift. Jesus used a child as a model for the ultimate giver—one who is dependent on God. Preschoolers are sometimes more sensitive to God and His work in the world around them. Encourage preschoolers to give in ways they are able.

Half-truth **Preschoolers are resilient and rebound easily.**

Preschoolers can overcome great odds, but churches frequently use this ability as an excuse for overcrowded departments with limited numbers of trained teachers and few necessary resources for effective teaching. When appropriate ratios are maintained, relationships develop more easily. Strong relationships provide avenues for guiding a child's spiritual growth and behavior. At times, what is described as *resilience* in a child may simply be a lack of skills to communicate needs. In times of crisis or death, much attention may be paid to adults, but frequently preschoolers are neglected. Again, strong relationships between teachers and preschoolers encourage communication, understanding, and support.

Myth **Preschoolers begin to learn about God when they begin to talk.**

Research demonstrates that at birth a child has already made some basic assumptions about life and those around him. Those beliefs continue in the years ahead. The first two years are critical. You may ask the question, "What can young preschoolers learn about God?" They can learn a lot! For a child this age, the parents and teachers at church become representatives of who God is. The child begins to learn about a God whom he cannot see by his relationships with people he can see. A word of caution: The concrete of the first foundational concepts sets and dries quickly, and once dried, must be broken to be reshaped. The first and foremost thing young preschoolers learn about God is that He loves them. They understand this concept before their first word is spoken. They understand love not by mere words, but by actions. Yet, when words like *God, Jesus,* and *Bible* are used early and frequently with a young preschooler, and when they are associated with loving and engaging activities, the words are bound forever into the preschooler's ears and mind.

Myth **God only works within understood stages of development.**

The general characteristics of each year of life provide guideposts for teachers and parents in planning ways to teach preschoolers the Bible. However, do not confuse general characteristics with hitching posts. God works with preschoolers as well as adults on an individual basis. A teacher who is committed to young children and their spiritual growth will not force them beyond their limitations, but will strive to know their individual levels of learning. Jesus took His disciples at their individual levels and moved them forward to deeper relationships with Him. Foundational teaching that leads to spiritual conversion considers the individual and tailors a teaching plan that encourages spiritual growth.

Half-truth **The spiritual development of preschoolers is the church's responsibility.**

The church does share some responsibility for the spiritual growth of children, but the Bible is clear about the role of the home as the center of biblical instruction. In looking to the Old Testament for a model, it is clear that preschoolers were almost never taught at church. Toward the end of Old Testament history, synagogues were springing up outside Jerusalem, and boys around the age of six went to religious school. Even then, the church only provided a supportive role in the biblical instruction of preschoolers and children. In looking at today's society, the home is still the best place. The most faithful churchgoers attend only 37 times a year. A child in the average household experiences 35 hours a week of television and other media. The impact of the church is limited. Parents must be the primary Bible teachers or faith will not be an important part of a child's life. The trap some churches fall into is assuming a false sense of total responsibility while parents neglect *their* responsibility. No amount of time spent in Sunday School, Christian school and day care, or parachurch Bible study groups replaces the impact of parents on a child's faith. Churches must seek to partner with parents to affect preschoolers. Churches must change a parent in order to change a child.

Half-truth   **Teaching young children is a woman's responsibility.**
The responsibility of teaching young children belongs to both men and women. However, in many churches today, a child might go years before seeing a man teaching at church. What an unsettling thought! Think about the early implications for young boys and girls. Does this mean the only people who work and teach for God at church are women? God placed men and women in the family. God placed men and women in the church. Each gender brings a different and essential dimension to the teaching of young children. Where there is no model, there will likely be no example to follow. Boys and girls need to see dads and moms and men and women involved in teaching and leading at church.

These myths and half-truths are fairly easy to describe and identify but are difficult to eliminate. A first step is to understand where you are in this process. Take a few moments to describe your philosophy of teaching foundational biblical truths to preschoolers.

Biblical Concepts—First Steps Toward Faith: Building a Biblical Worldview

One way to better understand teaching biblical truths is to recognize the foundational theological concepts that are suitable and necessary for each age level. Review these nine biblical concept areas. The chart on pages 12-13 represents the first stages of building a biblical worldview. A more comprehensive document is used for all ages in order to develop Bible study resources for individual age groups and for the family. Recognizing these biblical foundations and acting on them by one class or even one organization is a step in the right direction. However, to impact the child in the most meaningful way, a church must evaluate its total ministry to preschoolers. Sunday School, children's choir, Mission Friends, Discipleship Training, Vacation Bible School, and church weekday education must strive toward a biblical foundation for ministry to preschoolers, their families, and their teachers.

Setting priorities in the church is important. In Matthew 6:33, Jesus taught that the first priority in a follower's life is to seek the kingdom of God. In the New Testament, we can find an outline of God's way for building His kingdom through five functions of the church: evangelism, discipleship, fellowship, ministry, and worship. When these functions are followed, there are four growth results: numerical, spiritual, ministry expansion, and mission advance.

Use this checklist to evaluate your church's teaching ministry to preschoolers.

___ Does your church include older preschoolers in corporate worship?

___ Does your church choose hymns or choruses from time to time that are understandable for older preschoolers?

___ Does your pastor visit with preschoolers both in group settings and casually at church?

___ Does your church place a priority on enlisting and training preschool teachers? How frequently does your church provide training?

___ Does each program provided for preschoolers meet the biblical foundations for teaching preschoolers?

___ Is your preschool teaching space clean and uncluttered? Does it provide enough space for preschoolers to move and learn (35 square feet per child)? Or is it a place filled with adult cabinets, chairs, desks, and tables?

___ Are preschoolers allowed to choose from a variety of Bible-learning centers/activities in order to learn in the way God has gifted them?

___ Does your church think of ways to include older preschoolers in worship and other important functions?

___ Does your church feature a welcome center for preschoolers or include training for greeters to welcome preschoolers and help in transition?

___ Does your church provide for at least two adult teachers in each room at all times?

___ Does your church have a security system for receiving and releasing preschoolers?

___ Does your church practice universal precautions in the area of hygiene and safety?

___ Does your church have men and women teaching in each department?

___ Does your church provide teaching activities for preschoolers as young as babies?

___ Does your church have a *First Contact* or Cradle Roll ministry?

___ Is a true learning opportunity provided every time a preschooler is at church?

The goal of foundational teaching may never be fully attained for every child, but teachers must never stop trying. The benefits are too great, and failure is eternal.

While we have made great strides toward our goal, we have a great distance to go. Part of that distance is in educating our teachers, pastors, and churches about the biblical foundations for teaching preschoolers. You may want to plan a time with your church staff to promote and educate your church about its preschool ministry. .

Remember, a church needs to hear positive things about preschoolers. Frequently, churches see preschool ministry as a fund-raising drive. The only time you hear from them is when there is a need. Find ways to incorporate information about preschoolers throughout the year and create an awareness of your church's ministry to preschoolers.

	Younger Preschooler	Middle Preschooler	Older Preschooler
BIBLE	• God is good. • God made you. • God loves me. • God hears me. • God helps me. • God loves people.	• God is good. • God made everything. • God loves people and is with them. • God hears people pray. • God helps people. • God shows His love to people. • God loves people even when they make wrong choices. • God tells people to sing and pray to Him. • God tells people to do what He says. • God can do all things. • God does what He says He will do. • God knows everything. • God is real.	• God is good. • God created everything. • God is always with people. • God hears people pray. • God helps and provides for people. • God shows His love to people. • God loves people even when they make wrong choices. • God tells people to worship Him. • God tells people to obey Him. • God can do all things. • God always keeps His promises. • God knows everything. • God is real, the only true God.
JESUS	• Jesus was born. • God chose a family for Jesus. • Jesus grew like me. • Jesus learned about God. • Jesus told people about God. • Jesus helped people because He loved them. • Jesus loves me. • Jesus did everything God told Him to do. • Jesus is alive.	• God sent Jesus to earth. • Angels told Mary and Joseph that Jesus would be born. • Jesus grew like me and had a family. • Jesus learned about God by reading the Scriptures. • Jesus taught people what God is like. • Jesus healed sick people. • Jesus loves people. • Jesus is God's Son. • Jesus always obeyed God. • Jesus is with God.	• God sent Jesus to earth as a real person. • People in the Old Testament told that Jesus would be born. • Jesus grew, learned, and had friends. • Jesus prayed to God. • Jesus taught people what God is like. • Jesus performed miracles. • People who love Jesus want to obey Him. • Jesus died on the cross and is alive. • Jesus is God's one and only Son. • Jesus was tempted to sin but did not. • Jesus is in heaven with God.
HOLY SPIRIT	Concept statements from the God concept area lay a foundation for later learning about the work of the Holy Spirit. Examples of those statements are • God helps me. • God loves me.	Concept statements from the God concept area lay a foundation for later learning about the work of the Holy Spirit. Examples of those statements are • God helps people. • God shows His love to people. • God loves people and is with them.	Concept statements from the God concept area lay a foundation for later learning about the work of the Holy Spirit. Examples of those statements are • God helps and provides for people. • God shows His love to people. • God is always with people.
BIBLE	• The Bible is a special book. • The Bible tells about God. • People in the Bible told about God. • The Bible tells about Jesus. • The Bible helps me know what to do.	• The stories in the Bible really happened. • The Bible teaches us what God is like. • People in the Bible wrote about God. • The Bible teaches what Jesus did. • The Bible teaches right and wrong.	• Everything in the Bible is true. • The Bible teaches us what God and Jesus are like. • People wrote God's words in the Bible. • The Bible teaches that Jesus died on a cross. • The Bible teaches right and wrong.
SALVATION	• God loves us. • God cares about us.	• God sent Jesus because He loves us. • God sent Jesus because He cares about us. • People sometimes make wrong choices.	• God sent Jesus to help people because He loves them. • God sent His only Son, Jesus, because He cares about us. • People sometimes choose to disobey God.

Building Biblical Foundations

** CREATION**		
• God made day, night, plants, sky, sun, moon, stars, animals, water, birds, fish, and people. • God made people. • God made food for people and animals. • God planned for people to care for the things He made. • God wants me to enjoy the things He made. • God wants me to thank Him for the things He made.	• God created the world in six days and rested on the seventh. • God made people different from the other things He made. • God provides for His creation. • God planned for people to care for the things He made. • God wants me to enjoy the things He created. • God wants me to thank Him for the things He made.	• God created the world in six days and rested on the seventh. • God created people able to make choices. • God provides for His creation. • God planned for people to care for the things He made. • God wants me to feel a sense of wonder as I enjoy the things He created. • God wants me to praise Him for His creation.
** CHURCH**		
• People learn about God and Jesus at church. • People at church love me. • People at church help me. • People at church sing, talk to God, and listen to Bible stories.	• People learn about God and Jesus at church. • People at church love each other and teach about God and Jesus. • People at church help others. • People at church worship by singing, talking to God, and listening to Bible stories. • People give money at church. • Jesus had a special meal with His friends. • The Bible has stories about baptism.	• The church is people who gather to learn about God and Jesus. • Church helpers teach about God and Jesus. • The church provides ways for people to help others. • People at church worship by praying, giving, singing, reading the Bible, and learning more about God and Jesus. • People give money at church to help others learn about God and Jesus. • The Lord's Supper is a special meal to remember Jesus. • A person is baptized after he or she becomes a Christian.
** PEOPLE**		
• God made me. • God made me special. • God created me to make choices. • God helps me learn. • God loves for me to talk to Him. • God helps me grow like Jesus grew. • God wants me to be a friend. • God loves me. • God has plans for me. • God helps me. • God helps me learn about Jesus.	• God helps me grow. • God made me, so I am special. • God allows me to make right and wrong choices. • God made me able to think, work, and play. • God loves for me to pray. • God helps me grow like Jesus grew. • God helps me to be kind to my friends. • God will always love me. • God has a plan for people. • God helps me do what He says. • God wants people to take care of their bodies. • Jesus taught that I can tell others I'm sorry when I hurt them. • God wants people to learn from Jesus.	• People grow as God planned for them to grow. • People are special because God made them. • God allows people to make right and wrong choices. • God made people able to do many things well. • God wants people to pray. • People can try to be like Jesus. • Jesus taught how God wants us to treat other people. • No matter what happens, God loves people. • God has a plan for every person. • People can show love for God by obeying Him. • God wants people to take care of their bodies. • God helps me obey Him. • Because Jesus forgives, I can tell others I'm sorry for hurting them. • God wants people to follow Jesus' example.
** FAMILY**		
• God made families. • Families love one another. • God gave me a mommy and daddy to help me. • My family tells me about God. • God made families. • God loves families.	• God's plan for families is in the Bible. • God wants family members to love and help one another. • God's plan is for children to do what their parents tell them to do. • Families talk to God and read the Bible. • God's plan for families is found in the Bible. • God loves families even when bad things happen.	• God's plan for families is for mothers and fathers to raise children. Children are born or adopted into families. • God wants families to show love, respect, and kindness to one another. • God's plan is for children to obey their parents. • Families worship God together. • Families are made when people marry. The marriage of Adam and Eve shows us God's plan. • God loves families even when they hurt each other, and He wants families to forgive each other.
** COMMUNITY AND WORLD**		
• God made people. • God helps people. • People tell others about God and Jesus. • People can talk to God. • God cares about other people and me.	• God made people alike and different. • God helps people. • People tell others about God and Jesus. • People can pray for others. • People are important to God. • Missionaries are people who tell other people about God and Jesus.	• God made people alike and different, and all are special to Him. • God works through people. • People who love God tell others about Him all over the world. • People can pray for others in their communities and world. • The Bible tells me to love others in my community and world. • Missionaries tell people about God and Jesus in my country and in other countries.

Understanding the Preschoolers We Teach

Chapter 2

lark could give a teacher a great amount of joy or a great amount of difficulty. He gave me a great amount of joy. He was in my class of Mission Friends. Clark rarely chose to do art; he enjoyed puzzles. One month it was my turn to teach in the art center. I decided to try an unusual activity to see if Clark would choose to come to the art center. I collected a few small sink and commode plungers. I filled pie pans with small amounts of paint. The children could plunge paint onto large sheets of paper. The first child to try was Clark. He smiled from ear to ear. The entire time he painted, we talked about a missionary who lived in a country where people did not have water in their houses. Through the month, I tried other unusual art activities, mostly using large painting instruments. Clark was there every time. The reason Clark had never chosen to use crayons or small paintbrushes was because his body was not ready for that type of play.

Clark and I became good friends. When it was time for us to leave his church, I mourned over the lost future opportunities to observe his growth. He taught me a great deal about preschoolers. He also taught me that the child is the best indicator of what methods should be used in teaching. If we had forced Clark to paint with small paintbrushes or draw with crayons, he would have been unhappy and resistant to the message of the Bible. By allowing him to choose the methods he enjoyed, we were able to teach him far more effectively, and his behavior was far more acceptable.

Jesus offers the best model for teaching and relating to preschoolers. Read and consider the story of Zacchaeus in Luke 19:1-10.

Jesus took the time to find out about Zacchaeus. Jesus knew that Zacchaeus' lifestyle had alienated his friends, family, and community. So what did Jesus do when He encountered a person with no friends? He began by using Zacchaeus' name. He went to Zacchaeus' home which further built a relationship and demonstrated Jesus' commitment to know and love Zacchaeus.

Needs

Understanding preschoolers is crucial to teaching them and meeting their needs. Preschoolers come from many different backgrounds and situations, but they all have the same basic needs. These basic needs are love, trust, acceptance, independence, security, freedom, guidance, and a sense of accomplishment.

To a preschooler:

• *Love* is an action rather than an abstract feeling. When you smile, listen, hug, or spend time with a child, you communicate love to the child. A child expresses love as a result of how she has experienced love.

musical
logical
natural
physical
reflective
visual
verbal

• **Trust** is developed through relationships. Consistency is the key to successful trust building. The trust a child develops in the early years is the basis for faith and trust in Jesus when he is older. How can a child trust a God whom he can-not see if he cannot trust the people he can see? In the first years, teachers and parents become representatives of God. Because these children cannot read, adults are a living Bible.

• **Acceptance** grows from the unconditional love of parents and teachers. Because a child is made in God's image, she is worthy of acceptance and respect from the adults around her. When you listen and give a child undivided attention, you communicate your acceptance of the child even when the child's behavior is unacceptable. Be careful not to overemphasize a child's clothing or artwork. These messages can be perceived as a basis for acceptance. Saying to a child, "You used red and green. You really worked hard on that picture," is better than, "Sara, that is the best picture I have ever seen."

A biblical principle for teaching is to magnify relationships. The relationship between a child and a teacher becomes the power-ful connection between the child and the biblical truth.

• **Independence** is developed by giving a child appropriate choices. A preschooler needs the opportunity to discover the unique gifts and abilities God has given her. When you allow a child to complete a puzzle by herself, you foster independence in the child. Limited guidance by the teacher may be needed to ensure the child's success. Then the child can grow to be what God wants him to be. She also can begin to realize that God wants her to make right choices and has gifted her with the power to do so.

• **Freedom** is learning to make appropriate choices. When a child begins to make right choices, he realizes that more freedom is granted. When you guide a preschooler in making appropriate choices, you help the child develop independence. When you provide several different Bible-learning activities, you communicate freedom of choice to the preschooler. Remember, the goal of discipline is self-discipline. The child must grow in a way that fosters responsibility and wise decisions. Appropriate freedom creates a good track record of decision making on which preschoolers can draw in the future.

• **Security** means providing a worry-free environment where the child knows he is welcome, safe, and free from harm. A preschooler feels secure when he sees the same teachers and children in the same room following a familiar routine. Parents also need security. They need to know that their child is safe. A clean room with prepared teachers who use a security system to receive and release children allows parents to feel comfortable with the church.

• **Guidance** is direction given to help the child make choices. Through words, actions, and room arrangement, you guide the child to know how to care for himself, others, and property. Through discipline and guidance, you give a child the opportunity to learn right from wrong and make wise decisions on his own. As a result of this guidance, the child begins to develop self-discipline.

Correct a child's misbehavior by offering two positive options, give him an opportunity to make a wise choice. Also, allow preschoolers to live with appropriate consequences of their choices, such as : "Adam, you played with the blocks today. We need to pick them up. If you choose not to pick up the blocks, you will not have the choice of playing with them."

• *A sense of accomplishment* results from having been given opportunities to succeed. As a child develops and learns new skills, she gains a sense of accomplishment. Provide activities that challenge yet do not frustrate a child. In a class of three-year-olds, for instance, provide both 7-piece and 12-piece puzzles so that each child can succeed.

General Characteristics

Each child is a unique creation of God, created with a sense of awe and wonder about the world around him. Though each child is unique, he exhibits some characteristics common to all preschoolers.

A preschooler is *curious*. She learns by using all of her senses to explore the world around her. She wonders how the world works and what objects do. She investigates things that interest her. Threes often ask, "What?" Fours ask, "Why?" Fives ask, "How?"

A preschooler is *active*. Physical activity is part of the natural growth of a child. Provide a teaching environment that allows preschoolers to move around the room. If you ask a preschooler to sit still too long, learning may stop because all of the child's energy is focused on not moving.

A preschooler is *creative*. Enhance a child's imagination by providing an environment conducive to expression. Allow a child to express her own ideas and feelings by giving her a box of art supplies and blank paper rather than a coloring sheet.

A preschooler is *self-focused*. Why are preschoolers self-focused? Is it a bad characteristic that must be driven from a child? No, it is a gift from God in the early years. Because a child is self-focused, he tells adults when he is hungry, sick, or afraid. He can think about the world only from his own point of view. A two-year-old, for instance, may have difficulty sharing the puzzles in the room. As the child grows older, he has the opportunity to see adults model a caring, disciplined life. Then he will begin to act in ways that demonstrate a movement toward a self-disciplined life.

A preschooler is *sensitive*. Though she cannot verbalize her feelings, a preschooler can read the emotions and feelings around her. She needs a consistent, positive environment to help her grow. Without this type of environment, she may feel insecure and uncertain.

A preschooler has a *limited attention span*. His attention span is approximately one minute for each year of life. A child can only remain involved in an activity as long as his attention allows. Encourage each child to work at his own pace by providing a variety of activities. Then allow the child to choose and move among those activities. Be careful not to equate a limited attention span with limited learning. A limited attention span means that

To keep younger preschoolers secure, use masking tape or mailing labels for name tags. (A quick way to remember this is to label all things that relate to the child that begin with a "B." Label the baby, bottle, bag, bed, and blanket.) Name tags ensure that each baby receives his own food and other personal items.

Understanding the Preschoolers We Teach

teaching and learning must be focused. For active preschoolers who have limited attention spans, group time may not be the best way to teach the Bible story or Bible truths. Therefore, the biblical truth and Bible story should pervade the entire session through activities and Bible-related conversation. The child who only hears the story in group time has had a limited Bible-learning experience. The best teaching occurs when the child hears a portion of the Bible story as it relates to the child's present experience or activity.

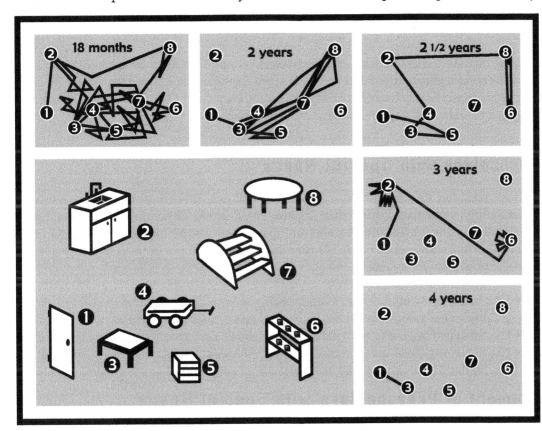

Observe the movement of each age child during a seven-minute time period. How does this information impact how teachers set up their rooms for teaching?

A preschooler is **literal-minded**. She thinks in terms of what she has seen and experienced. She understands words only in their concrete meanings. The use of symbolic or figurative language at home or church may confuse her. If a preschooler hears the phrase, "You have grown another foot," she will look to see where her new foot has grown. Speak in terms the child can understand the first time. Words that must be explained are not as easily remembered or used in a later context. As preschoolers mature toward kindergarten, begin using words that are interchangeable. For example, with babies, ones, and twos, the word *church* is used to refer to all places of worship. With kindergartners, interchange other words, such as *temple, tabernacle*, or *synagogue*. In this way, the child has a word that relates to his current experience. *God's Word* or *God's house* can be confusing to preschoolers of all ages. The words *Bible* and *church* may be more easily understood.

A preschooler **explores limits** for two reasons. First, he wants greater independence. Second, he wants to be reassured that his environment is safe. Frequently, preschoolers who push the limits do so because the limits are always moving and changing. When parents and teachers have different expectations for behavior, the child is confused and will automatically begin to search for the new boundaries. Parents and teachers must work together in having similar expectations. Teachers at church must do the same. What

17

is unacceptable in Mission Friends or preschool choir should be unacceptable in Sunday School. As the child questions limits in his learning experiences, provide firm but loving guidance to ensure safety and a secure environment.

In addition to these general characteristics, preschoolers have common age-group characteristics. The chart on pages 22-23 describes each stage of a preschooler's development and growth. Remember, however, that the rate of development varies from child to child. Each child moves through these stages at his own pace.

Understanding characteristics of preschoolers is important for choosing age-suitable curriculum and activities. Yet, even the best activities must be adapted to meet the individual needs of specific preschoolers. Discovering how each child in your class/department is gifted to learn will help you make these adaptations.

Preschoolers with Special Needs

Approximately 49 million Americans have disabilities. These disabilities cover a broad field, including mental handicaps, visual impairment, deafness or hearing impairment, learning disabilities, physical disabilities, and multiple disabilities. Mainstreaming or including preschoolers with special needs is easier during the preschool years than at any other age because of the way we teach.

Here are some general guidelines:
- Visit in the home of the child. Without being too intrusive, find out all you can about the child from the parents. What are their goals and wishes for the child?
- Use "child first language." Say, "a child with cerebral palsy" instead of "a cerebral palsy child."
- Use the words *challenged* or *disability* instead of *handicap* when discussing physical disabilities. However, *mentally handicapped* or *visually handicapped* is generally accepted.

Placement of Preschoolers with Special Needs

Place a preschooler with special needs in the same class with her peers. Enlist an additional teacher and adapt the teaching plan if necessary. In some cases, a child with special needs may be grouped with younger preschoolers, but a good rule to follow is that the child with special needs should not be more than two years older than the oldest child in the class.

There are three times when a child may need the constant attention of an individual teacher, whether in the department with his peers or in a separate department:
- the child's disabilities are so involved that he requires constant attention;
- the child has disruptive behavior that is totally inappropriate for his age; or
- the child's level of comprehension is far below that of his age group.

If parents and teachers decide together to place the child in a separate department, watch for ways to include the child with his peers.

Ways Preschoolers Learn

As you teach preschoolers biblical truths, keep in mind the eight basic ways all preschoolers learn. While preschoolers are unique and grow through the same stages at different rates, these eight basic ways preschoolers learn remain constant.

Senses—Preschoolers learn through their senses. Through touching, smelling, tasting, hearing, and seeing, preschoolers discover things God made. They use their hands, feet, eyes, noses, ears, and mouths as a part of the learning process. Watch for ways to appeal to all the senses, not just seeing and hearing. This type of teaching is worth the extra preparation and resources because its impact makes learning more memorable.

Curiosity—Exploring the world around us is a lifelong process. Curiosity in the adult world is evident in our space programs, science, technology, archaeology, and in many careers and fields of study. A preschooler's curiosity drives him to explore, discover, and ask the question, "Why?" Find ways to facilitate this exploration, taking the opportunity to shape the child's worldview by pointing to God, the Creator and sustainer of life.

"Hands-on" Experience—Today, the term "hands-on" is used to refer to anything a child can do. This idea leads to the misconception that keeping a child busy and involved is the end or goal of teaching. "Hands-on" truly means involving the child in an activity that leads the child to a greater understanding of a Bible truth. In "hands-on" teaching, preschoolers are guided through an activity toward a Bible truth that can be understood and applied in that moment and in the child's life.

Satisfaction—Should teaching at church be "satisfaction guaranteed?" Yes, this means the child is given choices that allow him to learn in the ways God has gifted him. Through gaining a sense of accomplishment, the child realizes he is unique and is created in the image of God. Satisfaction affirms the individual's importance to God and dependence on God for all good gifts.

Relationships—Relationships form the eternal connections between the child and the biblical truth. Adults use various translations, commentaries, and Bible dictionaries to understand the message of the Bible. For preschoolers who do not have the benefit of adult language, the relationship with their teacher becomes the living commentary on the Scripture. In reality, you represent God, His Word, and His power as you relate to preschoolers.

Imitation—Preschoolers follow the lead of adults in their lives. Long before a baby can understand the words of adults, she is understanding the actions of adults. Preschoolers learn to follow Christ's example by following paths adults choose.

Play—Playing and learning are inseparable in the lives of preschoolers. Play offers the greatest opportunity for Bible teaching. Through play, a child learns and applies important truths, learns to relate in positive ways to others, learns to accept responsibility, and learns to solve problems. But play is just activity unless the teacher is guiding the activity and discussion toward foundational biblical truths.

Repetition—The comment, "Not this Bible story again!" can be heard from some adults who teach preschoolers. The fact is that preschoolers need the repetition of Bible truths and Bible stories. The use of repetition allows preschoolers to gain more knowledge and application of the truths. It also allows them to feel more confident about the Bible study. As a child grows, so does his knowledge and understanding. Repetition allows the child to build on previous foundational truths. If older preschoolers comment that they have heard the session's Bible story before, ask them to tell you what they already know about the story. Write their comments on a poster board; then, tell the story. Afterward say, "Now let's see what we remembered about the story." Place a check mark by each written comment as you review it.

The Bible story is a foundational element of any approach to learning or teaching. The stories of God form the core of all learning that leads to foundational teaching and spiritual transformation. The biblical tradition of telling the stories of God's work to generation after generation forms the beginning threads of the Old Testament. This oral tradition can be found today in preschool classes in churches. Whether dressing up and playing out a Bible story, creating a picture while hearing facts about a Bible family, or saying a thank-you prayer to God while tasting oranges, the story—God's story—is the content that prepares and changes lives.

In addition to these general characteristics, preschoolers develop various approaches to learning as they grow. Jesus understood this diversity within people. Because He knew God created people with different ways of learning and dealing with life situations, Jesus used a diversity of approaches during the same teaching situation. While God created every preschooler to be unique, preschoolers of all ages approach learning in one or more of the following ways: relational, musical, logical, natural, physical, reflective, visual, and verbal. Every adult has dominant approaches to learning, but preschoolers learn through multiple approaches, often simultaneously. During the preschool years, dominant approaches may be difficult to distinguish. They also may change as preschoolers move through different life stages. Therefore, provide a variety of approaches to learning the same Bible truth during a session. In this way, you will be guiding preschoolers to learn in the way God created them to learn.

Approaches to Learning

Relational
These preschoolers are highly social. They make friends easily and may be very good talkers. They are keen observers of other children and adults, noticing their moods and motivations. Because relational children recognize how people feel, they are able to respond accordingly. They are drawn to activities that allow them to cooperate and interact with others. These children may grow to be known as "people persons."

Musical
Most preschoolers enjoy musical experiences. Yet some preschoolers from birth seem more sensitive to rhythm and pitch than others. They tend to be good listeners. Because they are more comfortable with music, singing and movement are their natural responses to music. These preschoolers may learn new songs quickly and remember them easily. They find it easy to express themselves through music—making up their own songs, playing instruments, and performing for others.

Logical

Problem solving is an enjoyable experience for some preschoolers. They see patterns in the world and can reason through difficult situations. They enjoy games and puzzles. They quickly understand the concepts of "less than" and "same as." These children will want step-by-step explanations with details. As older preschoolers, these learners may enjoy brain teasers or problem solving.

Natural

These preschoolers enjoy the beauty of God's creation. They can easily learn to identify the elements of the natural world. They may relate well to stories in the Bible that allude to elements in nature. Investigation and exploration of God's world are appealing to them. They have a fascination for plants and animals and a high sensitivity for taking care of God's world.

Physical

Preschoolers who approach learning from a physical standpoint are very active and may have good coordination. When a physical learner tells a story, she not only tells it, she plays it out. Physical learners also may be inclined to learn through mission projects or other helping activities. They like to use their physical abilities and skills in games and dramas. They do not just use their minds to learn; they use their entire bodies.

Reflective

Reflective learners tend to understand who they are and how they feel. Working alone may be their desire. Preschoolers who have this approach to learning do not shun the company of children but often choose activities that allow self-expression. These preschoolers also are comfortable with extended periods of solitude. They may internalize concepts by personalizing them.

Visual

Visual learners can "see" in their imaginations as well as in the concrete world. They enjoy creating their own pictures and visual representations of what they are learning. Interacting with teaching pictures is a preferred experience for these preschoolers. They hear stories and visualize the events through word pictures. Being visual learners does not mean that children will be drawn to creating art or will have specific gifts in creating art.

Verbal

Some preschoolers learn best through reading words (or being read to), writing (or dictating), speaking, and listening. Verbal learners like the sounds of words and may have large vocabularies. Preschoolers with this approach to learning like to talk and play word games. They enjoy stories, poems, and jokes.[1]

[1] Adapted from Thomas Armstrong, *7 Kinds of Smart: Identifying and Developing Your Many Intelligences* (New York: Thomas

Characteristics of Preschoolers

	Babies	Ones	Twos
Physical	• use many complex reflexes • begin to reach toward objects • hold up their heads • sit without support • roll over, crawl • look for dropped toys	• sit well in chairs • climb • love to explore • use markers on paper • carry objects from place to place • move constantly	• develop preference for right or left hand • stand on one foot and balance • jump on tiptoes • walk between parallel lines • have better gross motor coordination • have difficulty relaxing • help undress self
Mental	• use senses to learn • cry to signal pain or distress • recognize principle caregivers • use vocal and nonvocal communication • react differently to familiar and unfamiliar • know and respond to name	• remember simple events • begin to group familiar objects • use trial and error in learning • can label body parts • understand and use words for items • try to make self understood	• use 5 to 300 words • begin using sentences • identify self by gender • follow simple directions • match, compare, group, and sort items • enjoy repetition • begin using numbers • repeat songs • know colors
Social/Emotional	• show alertness when talked to • smile broadly at others • begin to initiate social interchange • become quiet in unfamiliar settings • make eye contact • are interested in other children	• experience stranger anxiety • play simple games • can practice "taking turns" • like to exert control • recognize others' emotions • imitate household actions	• take interest in family • try to help • initiate play with peers • can be loving and affectionate • are responsive to others' moods • use imagination • strongly assert independence
Spiritual	• develop a sense of trust as needs are met consistently • sense attitudes and expressions of love • learn to associate God's name with love and trust • sense importance associated with Jesus and the Bible • may point to the Bible and pictures of Jesus	• begin to make simple choices • continue to grow in trust of adults • begin to distinguish between acceptable and unacceptable behavior • begin to recognize simple pictures of Jesus	• can sing simple songs about God and Jesus • can say thank you to God • can listen to Bible stories

Threes	Fours	Pre-Ks	Kindergartners
• use large muscles • dress self fairly easily • display some fine motor skills • notice the differences in boys and girls • dislike nap time and cannot sleep during this time	• show good large muscle coordination • develop a longer, leaner body • develop fine motor control for cutting with scissors, painting, and drawing • walk backwards • need a high level of physical activity	• show good eye-hand coordination • dress themselves • exhibit right- and left-handedness • control their large muscles • enjoy building materials with parts to assemble • are learning to print and copy words	• skip well; hop in a straight line • display good eye-hand coordination • cut well with scissors • exhibit well-established right- or left-handedness • begin cutting permanent teeth • girls may display more maturity than boys
• use 300 to 1000 words • learn short songs • display creativity and imagination • experience fears and bad dreams • begin speaking in complete sentences • do one thing at a time • want to know what things are and how they work	• remember name and address • have increased attention span • can do two things at once • are imaginative; cannot separate fact and fantasy • show a curiosity about life cycle • understand time concepts better • use 500 to 2000 words	• are challenged by new tasks • seek explanations concerning why and how • begin to recognize basic reading words • enjoy classification, sequencing, and sorting • use many words without knowing their meanings • use a vocabulary of 2000 plus words	• begin to print name • know colors and shapes • can name most uppercase letters • can read a few words • utilize a 2000 word vocabulary • say numbers 1 to 20 • know morning from afternoon • hear the beginning sounds of words
• try to please adults; conform more often • can show self-control, but resort to temper tantrums when angry • take turns more readily • like to hear own voice • respond to verbal guidance and enjoy encouragement • play with others • have imaginary friends	• have total confidence in own abilities • are bossy; show great independence • tattle frequently • focus on cooperative play and take turns • like to be helpers if they initiate the idea • respond to reason, humor, and firmness	• play cooperatively with other children • enjoy imitating adults • begin to distinguish truth from untruths • enjoy competition • are learning to share and take turns • can accept responsibility	• work in small groups • comfort upset friends • have best friends, but change friends often • like to please adults • may be prone to self-criticism and guilt • enjoy group play • play easy games with a friend, following rules • may continue to express fears
• can identify some Bible characters and stories • enjoy singing songs • understand that God, Jesus, the Bible, and church are special • try to please adults • begin to understand consequences of behavior: may feel embarrassed	• like to retell Bible stories • enjoy Bible verse games • recognize that God and Jesus love people and help people in special ways • accept responsibility for helping people • begin to develop a conscience	• ask questions about God • express love for God and Jesus • can recall Bible stories • can make life application of Bible verses • show concern for others • can sing songs about Jesus • continue to develop a conscience	• like to tell Bible stories • use the Bible to find Bible phrases/verses • like to know they are doing what the Bible says • sing songs about God and Jesus • help and love others • take care of God's world • continue developing a conscience and express guilt

Getting Into Focus:
Partnering with Parents

Chapter 3

Preschool Sunday School, choir, church weekday education, Mission Friends, and Discipleship Training focus on what is best for the child. Resources are developed with the child in mind. Teachers are trained with the child in mind. Rooms are planned with the child in mind. Our goal is to guide the child to take steps toward conversion and spiritual transformation.

Yet all the programs in the world cannot take the place of godly parenting. All preschool ministry programs should strive to reach the parents as well as preschoolers. The greatest teaching on Sunday morning cannot replace the impact of parents. A literacy and English as a second language teacher was asked, "What is the most determining factor in success?" The teacher responded, "In order to teach a child English, you must teach a parent English." These words remind preschool teachers of the same principle. In order to guide a child toward conversion and spiritual transformation, we must witness to parents, mentor parents, and hold them accountable for their responsibility as their children's primary Bible teachers.

As teachers, we spend a great deal of time planning and preparing for the child to arrive. Yet we must realize that the child comes with a parent who not only controls the child's attendance pattern, but also has a major influence over the child's life and development. This observation does not mean that we begin to gear teaching or room setup to appeal to parents. Rather, it means we build a relationship with the parents before and after the session. It means we attempt to influence and encourage parents in their role. Simply put, we cannot focus completely on the child to the exclusion of the parents. In order to truly focus on the child, we must focus on the parents as well.

The Bible presents a clear picture of God's plan for teaching children spiritual truths. This biblical plan begins at home. Church attendance is simply not enough to lay foundations for faith. Deuteronomy 6 offers some practical guidance for parents as the primary teachers of biblical truths. Moses told the people: "The commandments I give you today must be in your hearts. Make sure your children learn them. Talk about them when you are at home. Talk about them when you walk along the road. Speak about them when you go to bed. And speak about them when you get up. Write them down and tie them on your hands as a reminder. Also tie them on your foreheads. Write them on the door frames of your houses. Also write them on your gates" (Deuteronomy 6:6-8, NIV).

Home—The Center of Biblical Instruction

- **What:** The Bible forms the core of how we teach babies through kindergartners about God. The Bible must be used with preschoolers from the very first days at home. It must be a centerpiece of play and worship in the home.

> ### A Great Idea
>
> Sometimes parents leave an upset child. When the child is having a better time at church, take an instant-print photo to give to parents after the session.

- **Who:** Parents must experience the biblical truth first. Parents cannot lead a child to experience the transforming truth of a passage until they first are transformed by its power.
- **Whom:** For children, the home is at the very center of biblical instruction. There is very little scriptural evidence of children being taught primarily in the tabernacle, synagogue, or temple. The home was the school of faith. The churches of those times supported the work of the home, not the other way around. No amount of Christian school, Sunday School, Discipleship Training, or church weekday education can replace the primary impact of the home on a child's spiritual development.
- **When:** Biblical instruction is not just family devotions. Family devotion time can be very meaningful; but, with a variety of ages represented, it is only the beginning of what Moses said. Many other times during the day offer opportunities for teachable moments with a child.
- **Where:** Anywhere and everywhere is the answer. In the daily grind of life, children are learning how to relate to God, even if that is not the parents' intention. So parents must develop ears and eyes that are sensitive to helping children recognize God at work in the world around them. This sense begins the process of a child's developing a biblical worldview.
- **Why:** Today, on average, the most active family comes to church 37 times a year. In one week children are exposed to 35 hours of television and other media.[1] To change a child, parents must experience a change and live out that change on a daily basis.
- **How:** The best way parents can teach biblical truths is to use the connection of relationships. The relationship parents have with their child is the best indicator of a child's relationship with God. If the relationship with the child is constantly rooted and built on God's Word, the child more likely will follow the model of his family.

> Teach the Bible in and through the family.

Who Are Today's Parents?

Most preschool parents are the same in many ways. In order to understand these parents, consider the following factors.

Factors that influenced parents' childhood:
- They were the most unprotected generation.
- Permissiveness without structure was the parenting philosophy of this time.
- Their parents were more focused on themselves than their children.
- This generation was the most aborted generation.
- 61% of mothers worked outside the home.
- One out of two marriages ended in divorce.

- These children averaged seven hours of television a day.
- Many of these children and teens became increasingly responsible for adult decisions.
- As teens, they experimented with sex, drugs, and violence.
- This generation has the highest incarceration in American history: 450 out of 100,000. That number is four times higher than in 1970.

General characteristics of this generation as adults:
- They hold a realistic view of life rather than an idealistic view of life.
- They achieved a high level of education in spite of failures in early years of education.
- They express high interest in spirituality but not necessarily religion.
- Practical approaches to problem solving are preferred over theoretical approaches.
- These young adults have learned from the mistakes of their parents. They are marrying later, having children later, and wanting to spend more time with their children.
- They are savvy and literate with multimedia and computer technology.
- These adults can handle multiple tasks at one time.
- As parents, they deeply care for their children and will strongly protect them.
- They are open to critique and evaluation.
- Eight percent contribute to a retirement plan—more than the previous generation.
- Forty percent invest in mutual funds.
- Traditional learning approaches are a turn off. They prefer "edutainment."
- They may have unrealistic expectations for their children.
- Their philosophy of life is "whatever works." [2]

> **Magnify relationships with preschoolers and parents.**

Implications for the church:
- This generation may view Bible study leaders as parents, thus desiring love and direction.
- These parents are looking for Bible studies and parenting helps that are practical.
- Mentors or role models may have a great degree of latitude in giving instruction or correcting behavior.
- As learners, these adults desire a strong purpose and a measurable outcome.
- In attending church, these church members may be sporadic and desire a variety of teaching and learning techniques, including multimedia.
- They value relationships over denominational or doctrinal issues.

Possibilities for preschool ministry:
- Offer parenting seminars that have specific outcomes and practical helps.
- Enlist and train parents as teachers and substitutes.
- Make visits in the home, modeling for parents how to teach at home.
- Make clear the benefits of regular attendance for the child.
- Build relationships through role modeling and hold parents accountable.

In what ways could you build a connection with parents of preschoolers at your church?

Making Contact

Make it your goal to be in each child's home at least once a year. During this visit, you may choose to:
- model a teaching opportunity with the child, either using the learner guide or another resource.
- deliver a learner guide or other resource to help parents teach the child at home.
- give a personal testimony about Sunday School and your salvation experience.

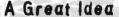

• share the FAITH presentation. (If you do not have FAITH training in your church, inquire with your pastor or minister of education.) The inside cover of all Sunday School leader guides and learner guides contains a plan for leading parents to Christ.

A Step of FAITH

Say: "In your personal opinion, what do you understand it takes for a person to go to heaven?" Listen to the parent's answer. If he has not had this life-changing experience, say: "Consider how the Bible answers this question. It is a matter of FAITH." Share this outline:

F is for FORGIVENESS

We cannot have eternal life and heaven without God's forgiveness.
"In Him [meaning Jesus] we have redemption through His blood, the forgiveness of sins" (Ephesians 1:7a, NKJV).

A is for AVAILABLE

Forgiveness is available.
It is available for ALL.
"For God so loved the world that He gave His only begotten Son, that whoever believes in Him should not perish but have everlasting life" (John 3:16, NKJV).
But it is not automatic.
"Not everyone who says to Me, 'Lord, Lord', shall enter the kingdom of heaven" (Matthew 7:21a, NKJV).

I is for IMPOSSIBLE

It is impossible for God to allow sin into heaven.
• Because of who He is: God is loving and just. His judgement is against sin. *"For judgement is without mercy"* (James 2:13a, NKJV).
• Because of who we are: Every person is a sinner. *"For all have sinned and fall short of the glory of God"* (Romans 3:23, NKJV).
But how can a sinful person enter heaven when God allows no sin? It is impossible.

T is for TURN

Turn means repent.
Turn from something—sin and self.
"But unless you repent you will all likewise perish" (Luke 13:3b, NKJV).
Turn to Someone; trust Christ only.
"If you confess with your mouth the Lord Jesus and believe in your heart that God has raised Him from the dead, you will be saved" (Romans 10:9, NKJV).

H is for HEAVEN

Heaven is eternal life.
Here: *"I have come that they may have life, and that they may have it more abundantly"* (John 10:10b, NKJV).
Hereafter: *"And if I go and prepare a place for you, I will come again and receive you to Myself; that where I am there you may be also"* (John 14:3, NKJV).

A Great Idea

Plan a pajama party for preschoolers to allow parents to do some Christmas shopping.

10 Ways to Ruin Relationships with Parents

1. *Arrive at church late and do not have the room prepared for teaching.* This habit communicates that preschoolers cannot learn and that their child is not valuable.
2. *Place continual advertisements in the church paper stating that there are not enough teachers in the preschool ministry.* This creates distrust in the preschool ministry. Vast announcements for workers rarely result in the type of leaders that are committed to teaching preschoolers in the long run.
3. *Fail to let parents listen as you greet the child. It is important to greet the child and begin teaching at the door.* Parents can see that you value their child in the first brief moments. They also can observe good examples of teaching and discover what the focus of the session will be. Also, try posting a message board that allows parents to see what will happen during the session.
4. *Write preschool policies so that they read like the State Department of Motor Vehicles Manual.* Most preschool policies are filled with "don't" statements, and they frequently fail to point out the benefits of the processes and procedures that they support. Example: "Don't bring a preschooler to church who has had a fever in the last 24 hours," rather than "In order to keep preschoolers healthy and help sick preschoolers recover, children who have had a fever in the past 24 hours should remain at home."
5. *Refer to the preschool area as the "nursery" and to teachers as "workers."* This may be only a matter of terminology, but most people outside the preschool area will understand these terms as caregiving, not teaching.
6. *Do not provide Bibles for use in preschool departments.* With all ages, the Bible must be included in every part of the session, even play. Babies need to associate the Bible with caring teachers who use words and phrases about God and Jesus. Three-year-olds need to see the teacher telling the Bible story from the Bible. Parents also need help with choosing a Bible for their child and how to use it at home. Preschoolers need a real Bible, not a storybook. The Bible must contain realistic illustrations so that the child does not confuse the Bible with fictional books.
7. *Do not visit prospects, inactive members, and active members.* Every preschooler needs a visit at least once during the year, and older preschoolers need a phone call or card every month.
8. *Do not be the child's advocate.* Preschoolers in most situations cannot speak for themselves. Parents will respect teachers who stand up for what is best for the child at home and at church.
9. *Critique the child in front of the parents.* Parents are sensitive about their child, even to the point that they may feel all of their child's behavior is a reflection of their parenting. Even though a child cannot understand every word of a conversation, he can understand emotions. Make an appointment to visit with parents if an issue is serious enough to merit a comment.
10. *Expect less from parents, and you will always get it.* Parents need teachers who care for them and their children. They need guidance and support.

A Great Idea

Take pictures of the children during the year. Make a photo album for each child of his experiences at church.

I was surprised to see Kathy and Dale coming to church again. A few weeks prior, they had announced to everyone that they were going to search for another church. They were disappointed in our pastor. I may have been surprised by their appearance, but what Kathy said next shocked me. She proceeded to tell me that she was interested in teaching Mission Friends. After discussing the possibility, I got the courage to ask about the reason for their return. Kathy, with an embarrassed look on her face, said that Eunice Ross calls every Saturday to talk to Austin, their four-year-old. Eunice is one of Austin's Sunday School teachers. She has been teaching four-year-olds for over 30 years. Kathy said that when the call came last Saturday, she was prepared to tell Eunice to take Austin off the roll. Kathy went through the story with Eunice, expecting to hear a very polite but sad reply. Instead, Eunice responded by asking, "Is Austin or your other child unhappy at church?" "Oh, no!" Kathy responded. What Kathy heard next was not exactly what she expected to hear from a 75-year-old Sunday School teacher. Eunice explained that a preschooler's need to feel acceptance and security at church is crucial to developing faith. She said that Kathy and Dale needed to consider the long-term needs of their children instead of their temporary unhappiness with the pastor.

I choked back a smile when the story became even more amusing. Eunice also told Kathy and Dale that they needed to start working at church. She told Kathy that it is easy to complain while sitting on the sidelines. In fact, Eunice used the words, "You get out what you put in." Kathy ended by saying she and Dale prayed about it and decided to give it a try. They knew our ministry to preschoolers was what their children needed.

While most of us would not be as bold as Eunice Ross, her example of loving ministry and mentoring is a fine model for us all. Parents today are often miles, even states, away from other family members. Their web of support usually only extends as far as the door of their mailbox. As Sunday School teachers and leaders, our opportunity to touch the life of a child can only truly be realized when we touch the life of a parent. Parents need individuals who are willing to minister, coach, and mentor.

---

[1] Catherine Stonehouse, *Joining Children on the Spiritual Journey* (Grand Rapids: BridgePoint, 1998), 23.

[2] Louis B. Hanks, *American Generations: The Churches in the 21st Century* (Nashville: The Sunday School Board of the Southern Baptist Convention, 1996).

Teaching Preschoolers the Bible

Chapter
4

eek after week, preschool teachers prepare Bible-learning centers/activities, leader pack items, group-time games, and Bible stories. In the process, they may get so involved in gathering supplies and arranging rooms that they miss the significance of their work. Most teachers judge the success of a session on the activities or the art that was created by the children. Artwork and other creations are temporary products that can never supercede the process of teaching and learning or the power of the relationship a teacher builds with a child around the Bible. Bible-learning centers/activities do not teach; teachers teach. This observation is true for Sunday School, Vacation Bible School, church weekday education, choir, Mission Friends, and Discipleship Training. Yet, in order for a teacher to teach, he must be taught. The job of a teacher is neither merely to convey Bible facts nor to create activities the child enjoys. A teacher first experiences personally the life-changing truth of the Bible text and then creates an experience that encourages the children to encounter the truth as well.

Teachers and parents also have the obligation and opportunity to create teaching and learning experiences that shape a child's worldview. Each child is developing a worldview of all that goes on around him. A child's worldview is similar to a pair of glasses that provides perspective and interpretation of the events, actions, and attitudes around the child. Through relationships, foundational biblical teaching, and the help of the Holy Spirit, teachers and parents can give the child a godly perspective on life from birth. This biblical worldview will help the child understand himself, others, the world, and God.

Bible teaching for preschoolers seeks to create an environment that leads teachers and parents to spiritual transformation; leads preschoolers toward a biblical worldview; and later in life, through foundational teaching, experience spiritual conversion. Bible teaching compels teachers and learners to live out and experience the biblical truths throughout the week. This is a seven-day-a-week strategy in which teachers prepare for the Bible teaching session, minister to preschoolers, witness to parents, and assist parents in their responsibility as the primary Bible teachers of their children.

The Essentials of Teaching for Spiritual Transformation

Seven-day-a-week Sunday School answers the following questions:
1. How does a teacher prepare to teach preschoolers biblical truths?
   Before the teaching session, teachers prepare by:
   experiencing a personal encounter with the Bible passage.
   creating a ministry environment.
   setting up the room.
   gathering resources for teaching foundational truths.

2. What should occur during the session to guide preschoolers toward understanding and acting on the biblical truth?

During the session, preschoolers encounter biblical truths by:

> telling the Bible story throughout the session.
> using Bible story conversation.
> providing three to five Bible-learning centers/activities.
> leading a group time for 3s through kindergartners.

3. What should occur at the close of the session and after the session to encourage week-long application of the biblical truth?

After the session, we continue to guide preschoolers toward foundational biblical truths:

> through encouraging parents to become the primary Bible teachers of their children.
> through providing parents with suggestions to follow up on the session during the week.
> through witnessing to developing a caring ministry to families.

Preparing to teach the Bible truth, helping preschoolers encounter the Bible truth, and helping parents to continue teaching throughout the week takes teaching the Bible to a new level!

Preschool teachers have only a limited time with preschoolers. The lesson begins with the session and continues following the session—for days, weeks, months, and even a lifetime! This can only happen when parents become the child's primary teachers.

Terms to Know in Your Leader Guide:

Bible Truth is a statement of the abiding truth that is the focus of a session.

Bible Verse or Phrase refers to the Bible verse or Bible phrase for the session.

Quick Plan provides teachers who have limited time or space with a simplified way to help preschoolers encounter Bible truths.

Life Application is a brief statement to guide leaders in planning a session that will have maximum application and integration for preschoolers and their families.

Prepare the Ministry Environment

The term *ministry environment* describes what takes place primarily during and after the Bible study session. The ministry environment includes the teaching/learning environment but also encompasses relationships among adults, preschoolers, and with God. The physical setting—including walls, chairs, visuals, and other equipment—is important, but Bible teaching requires a strong relationship between the teacher, parent, and child. Teachers should create an environment where everyone feels safe and interested in learning.

Depend on the Holy Spirit.

The ministry environment depends on the teacher's personal spiritual transformation. This transformation results from the teacher's relationship with God. Preparation of the ministry environment begins with prayer. The teacher should pray for preschoolers and their families daily. Prayer allows a teacher to depend on the Holy Spirit and to be open to God's movement in order to create a unique bond with families.

Teachers then should establish strong relationships with preschoolers to create an environment for learning biblical truths. The relationship a teacher has with the child often affects how well the child participates. The relationship is the glue that binds the biblical truth to the heart of a child. When preschoolers know they are loved and accepted, they will be more likely to be responsive to the teacher's guidance and to hearing Bible stories and Bible truths.

Bible Study

Teachers must prepare personally for God to use them to teach preschoolers the Bible. Teachers must ask God to speak to them personally. A portion of the leader guide gives teachers an opportunity to experience the Bible study before they teach it. Teaching preschoolers in a manner that leads to conversion and spiritual transformation is not a formula. The Holy Spirit works with each individual in a variety of ways during the course of life. In the lives of preschoolers, the Holy Spirit prepares the way for conversion later in life and spiritual transformation through foundational teaching at home and church. Preschool teachers must let God transform them first. Then they can teach from the overflow of what God is doing in their lives. Personal Bible study, training, and leadership meetings are opportunities God can use to transform teachers.

Before the Session
Teachers prepare for Bible teaching through personal Bible study by evaluating how their own lives are affected by the biblical content; how it relates to their lives; what God is saying to them; and to what extent they will live, trust, and obey God because of the Bible study. The personal Bible study process helps teachers prepare to teach preschoolers. This process guides teachers to explore the Scripture passage and commentary, asking key questions along the way. After teachers have experienced the Bible study for themselves, they look at the passage in terms of what God has to say to the preschoolers in their department. This process challenges teachers to go beyond conveying facts by identifying what truths within the Bible passage are foundational and meaningful for preschoolers.

Helping Preschoolers Discover the Bible Truth During the Session
What should happen during a session? For an adult, most learning experiences are sedentary. The simple fact is that God created children to move because moving is good for muscle growth, coordination, and brain development.

Bible-learning activities offer children the opportunity to move from place to place while learning the same content and Bible truths. By offering choices, teachers capitalize on the child's need to be active. Instead of working against the child's normal development, teachers are working with the child in learning Bible truths. Bible-learning activities provide a way for the child to choose his own way and pace of learning. Teachers guide the child's learning by choosing Bible-learning centers that focus attention on the Bible truths and Bible content for the session. Teachers can shape *what* a child learns by offering activities that appeal to *how* he learns.

Lead preschoolers to grow in responsibility for their actions and in learning about following Christ.

The age-group diagrams on pages 36-39 demonstrate what should occur during the session. Each diagram is similar to a time-lapse picture. All the activities/actions in the picture occur at different times or simultaneously during the session. The diagrams can help teachers see how children move, choose, and learn through Bible-learning activities. Using Bible story conversation with the preschoolers may be difficult at first. Sometimes teachers can be so focused on assisting a child in an activity that they fail to direct attention toward the Bible story and truth. From the moment the child arrives until he leaves, the focus of activities and conversation should be on the Bible story and truth.

Here are some examples of Bible story conversation:
As preschoolers arrive, invite them to guess the name of a plastic animal in a paper sack. When they guess, comment: "Do you know who named all the animals first? Adam did. Today, we are going to hear about Adam and Eve."

As a child paints at an easel in the art center, comment: "You are painting with beautiful colors. Joseph's father gave him a beautiful coat to show him how much he loved him."

As the child in the block/construction center moves a block boat across a large piece of blue paper (created to look like water), comment: "Jesus wanted to teach people about God, but there were too many people. Jesus decided to get in a boat. He had the disciples move the boat out a little way from shore. Then Jesus taught the people."

As a baby looks at a flower, sing: "God made flowers. God made flowers. God made the flowers, and God made Sarah."

Answering Preschoolers Questions
Preschoolers are very curious. Teachers must be prepared to answer their questions and guide them as they struggle with new thoughts. Teachers can support a child's growing understanding of the truths of the Bible by answering questions. Some questions may not have easy answers and may merit the honest response, "I don't know." Here are some guidelines for answering questions:
- Answer only what the child asks. A child will ask additional questions if she needs more information.
- Clarify rather than jumping to conclusions. Ask follow-up questions such as: "What makes you ask that question? Tell me more about your question." A child may ask, "Why did Andy get baptized?" This question may be only a request for information, not a request for a gospel presentation. Children incorporate concepts and information over time. Asking questions allows them to gain information, correct misconceptions, and gain new insights. Gaining biblical truths that lead to becoming a Christian is just one part of the process. The child must grow to understand through the work of the Holy Spirit that he is lost and separated from God. Becoming a Christian is more than having a desire or saying the right answers. It is the result of

God-led conviction. This conviction comes at different times in a person's life. For many people this occurs in middle to late childhood; but God works with individuals, so His timing is individual. Kindergarten-aged children who are active in church frequently ask questions about conversion. It is essential to use these times as steps in a journey that will eventually lead to accepting Christ as Savior.

- Speak in clear terms that a child can understand. Do not use adult symbolic language to explain concepts. Preschoolers are learning at a very fast rate, but they do not possess an adult's reasoning capabilities.

Choosing the Right Bible-learning Activity

Sometimes the greatest teaching moments come when the child is involved in an activity, and the child takes it to a different level. The child is more open to hearing the life-changing truths of the Bible. Bible-learning activities should help the child feel good about himself and confident about his God-given abilities. Activities must challenge the child. Finding the right balance between challenging and too difficult will help the child feel a strong sense of accomplishment related to his Bible-learning experience. Use the following questions to evaluate each activity you offer preschoolers:

Does the child have choices? Allowing a child to choose from several Bible-learning activities allows him to learn in the ways God has gifted him. When he learns in the ways God has gifted him, he is more teachable, open to learning, and well behaved.

Will the teacher accept the child's work? Avoid evaluating a child's work as good or bad. When a child enjoys an activity, she will not need excessive praise for her work. Rather, say: "You are working hard on that picture, I can see you enjoy painting."

Does the activity provide opportunities for developing relationships? The process in an activity is far more important than the final product. Provide activities that encourage relationship building between teacher and child and child with child.

Is the child allowed to move and play? Second only to the Bible and relationships, movement and play are the brick and mortar of teaching preschoolers the Bible. Frequently, preschoolers learn the most in activities that require a varying degree of movement.

Does the activity relate to the purpose of the session? Any activity can be a Bible-learning activity if the teacher is prepared to use Bible-related conversation with the child. However, a teacher must choose activities that naturally flow toward the Bible story and truth. The key word is *naturally*. Use activities that are easy for preschoolers to understand, such as, showing them a flower and saying, "God made the flower." While they may seem to enjoy object lessons, preschoolers usually do not understand them.

Does the activity distract from learning? Flannel graphs or child-made puppets can be great for Bible recall, but not to tell the Bible story. Preschoolers can become distracted by these, or even teaching pictures that are held up during the Bible story. Tell the Bible story with the Bible open, looking at the children. Then use pictures, child-made puppets, or flannel graphs to allow the children to retell the story. Remember Bible stories are about real people doing real things. Using a fictitious or cartoon puppet could confuse the child. .

Bible-learning Centers

* Homeliving/ Dramatic Play
* Art/Creative Art
* Puzzles/ Manipulatives
* Nature/ Science
* Blocks/ Construction
* Toys
* Books
* Music (depending on the age group of the preschoolers)

Use the Bible with preschoolers and parents.

Is the activity for the benefit of the child, parent, or teacher? The temptation is to choose activities that look good and cause parents to brag on the child or the teacher. It is not what a child *makes* that is eternal. It is what a child *learns* that is eternal.

Is the activity artificial or superficial? This is a trap for teachers. The activity must have a direct correlation or implication for Bible teaching.

The Bible-learning activities guide preschoolers to learn what the Bible means. Think about the last time adult Bible study was meaningful to you. What made that Bible study meaningful? This question is normally answered with the following statements:
- It met a need.
- It was applicable to my life.

If a preschooler could answer this question in adult terms, he would probably give the same answers. *Teachers must move beyond the facts of a Bible story and use the Bible to meet life needs, teach life application, and integrate the biblical truth into life.*

An understanding of what is foundational and what is useful to the child at each age and level of development is essential when considering what to teach preschoolers. Laying a foundation of biblical truths is not random or haphazard. Each concept and experience must build on previous understanding. Foundational teaching occurs within a learning context. Biblical concepts must relate to the whole of Scripture and the whole of life. If they do not, it is like giving preschoolers a brick of content, followed by another brick, followed by another brick, followed by another brick, until at some point teachers and parents assume they have strong foundation. But instead they have only a pile of bricks, and they do not have it for long.[2]

Helping Parents Continue to Guide Preschoolers Toward the Bible Truth
One of the goals of a teacher should be to help the child and the parents experience the biblical truth throughout the remainder of the week.

Connect the Bible Study with the Child
- The teacher could encourage kindergartners to do something during the week like a mission project or a family activity.
- The teacher could phone a preschooler during the week and continue Bible story conversation or Bible-related conversation.

Connect with the Parents: Parents are the primary Bible teachers. The teacher has opportunities to give tangible ways to parents to follow up on the session. This also gives the teacher opportunities to raise the accountability of parents for Bible teaching.
- Teachers could write notes on weekly pages about an activity for the parents to do at home.
- Teachers could phone parents with a creative idea for teaching the biblical truth at home.

Teachers who overlook this week-long emphasis will limit the impact of Bible truths on the lives of preschoolers and their families.

[1] Roy Edgemon and Barry Sneed, *Jesus By Heart* (Nashville: LifeWay Press, 1999), 10.
[2] Adapted from Alfie Kohn, *Punished by Rewards* (New York: Houghton Mifflin, 1993), 216.

Nursing Area

Crib

Crib

Babies and ones feel special when you smile and talk to them.

"I am glad to see Sarah today."

As child plays with a toy, open the Bible and say: "John loved God and told people about God's love."

Crib

Crib

Crib

Crib

Show a colorful flower and say: "See the flower? God made the flowers. God loves you."

Mat

"See the Bible, Sarah? The Bible tells us that God loves us."

Crib

Crib

Tap the book and show the pictures in the book *Things I See.*

Hold child so she can see God's creation through the window.

Window

Crib

Babies (Birth to One)

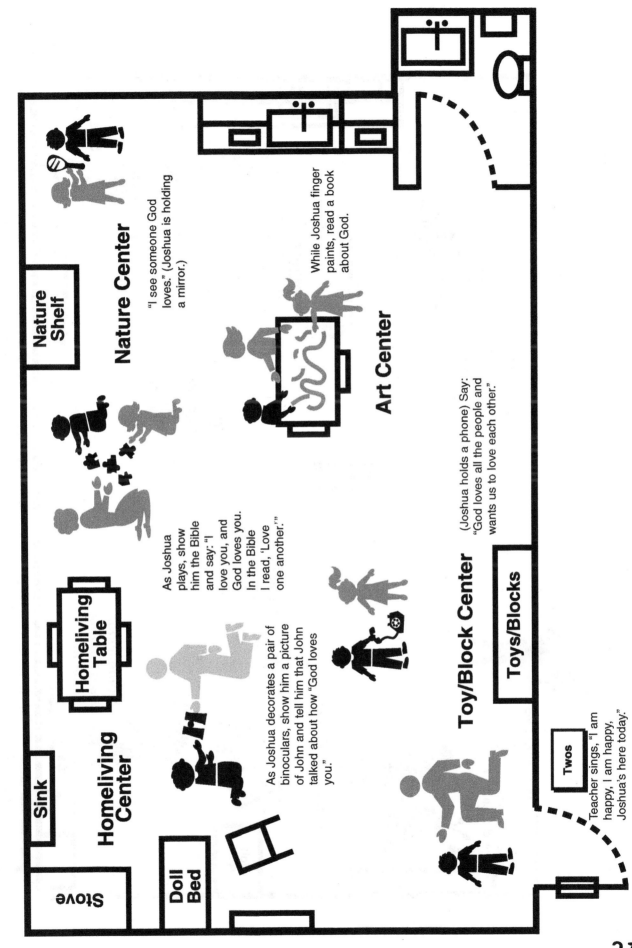

Nature Shelf

Nature Center

"I see someone God loves." (Joshua is holding a mirror.)

While Joshua finger paints, read a book about God.

Art Center

As Joshua plays, show him the Bible and say: "I love you, and God loves you. In the Bible I read, 'Love one another.'"

As Joshua decorates a pair of binoculars, show him a picture of John and tell him that John talked about how "God loves you."

(Joshua holds a phone) Say: "God loves all the people and wants us to love each other."

Toy/Block Center

Toys/Blocks

Sink

Homeliving Center

Homeliving Table

Stove

Doll Bed

Twos

Teacher sings, "I am happy, I am happy, Joshua's here today."

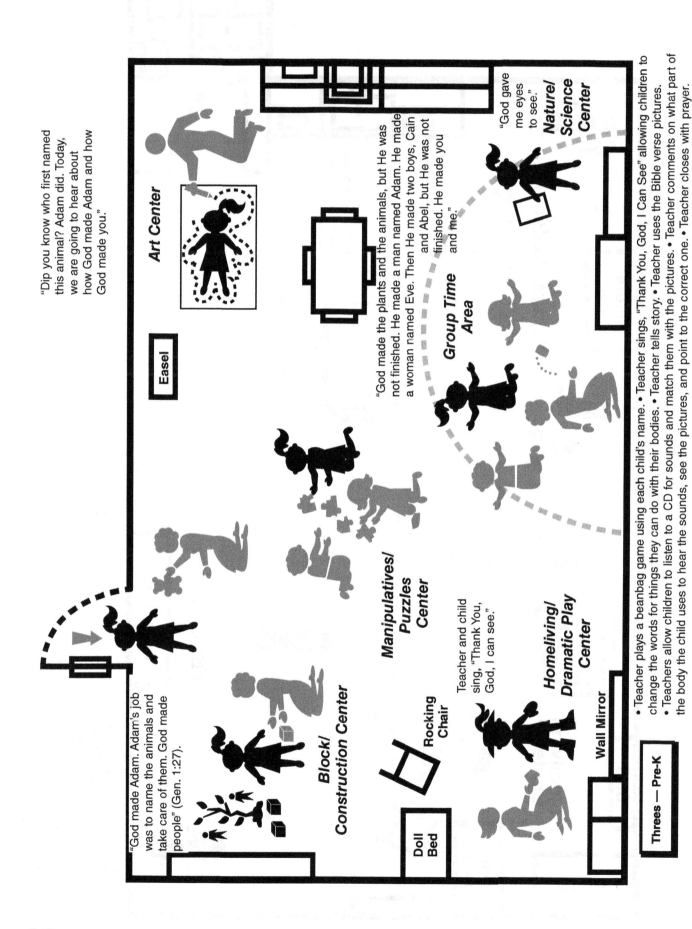

"Dip you know who first named this animal? Adam did. Today, we are going to hear about how God made Adam and how God made you."

Art Center

Easel

"God made the plants and the animals, but He was not finished. He made a man named Adam. He made a woman named Eve. Then He made two boys, Cain and Abel, but He was not finished. He made you and me."

"God gave me eyes to see."

Nature/ Science Center

Group Time Area

"God made Adam. Adam's job was to name the animals and take care of them. God made people" (Gen. 1:27).

Block/ Construction Center

Manipulatives/ Puzzles Center

Rocking Chair

Teacher and child sing, "Thank You, God, I can see."

Homeliving/ Dramatic Play Center

Doll Bed

Wall Mirror

Threes — Pre-K

• Teacher plays a beanbag game using each child's name. • Teacher sings, "Thank You, God, I Can See" allowing children to change the words for things they can do with their bodies. • Teacher tells story. • Teacher uses the Bible verse pictures. • Teachers allow children to listen to a CD for sounds and match them with the pictures. • Teacher comments on what part of the body the child uses to hear the sounds, see the pictures, and point to the correct one. • Teacher closes with prayer.

38

Teacher uses the activity. Children give each other envelopes with a message inside. Teacher shows the children the new words and tells the Bible story about John writing a letter. After the story, children review the story by using the Bible picture as the teacher asks, "Why did John write the letter?"

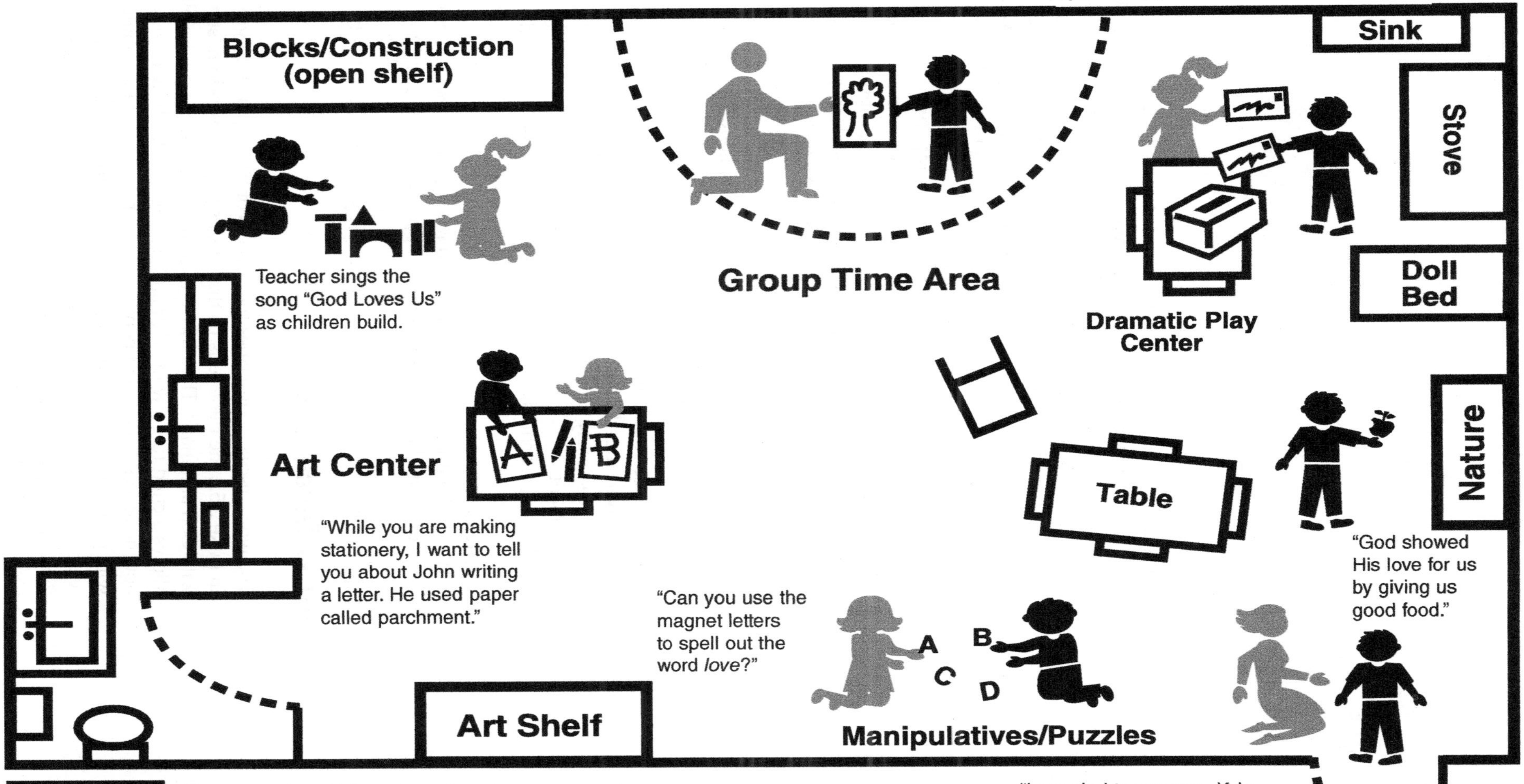

Blocks/Construction (open shelf)

Teacher sings the song "God Loves Us" as children build.

Art Center

"While you are making stationery, I want to tell you about John writing a letter. He used paper called parchment."

Art Shelf

After group time, Kyle and teacher sing a song and clap on each note. Kyle also reviews the Key Bible verse "God loves us" (1 John 4:7) on the weekly activity page.

Kindergarten

Group Time Area

Sink

Stove

Doll Bed

Nature

"Today we take a letter to the post office. In Bible times, when John wrote telling others about God's love, he sent his letter by another person."

Dramatic Play Center

"God showed His love for us by giving us good food."

Table

Manipulatives/Puzzles

"I am glad to see you, Kyle. Today we are learning about a man named John."

"Can you use the magnet letters to spell out the word *love*?"

39

Setting the Tone: Guiding Behavior

I taught four-year-olds in Sunday School. A few weeks before promotion, a teacher from the three-year-old department came in and commented: "Well, I see you have a block shelf in your room. Here is some advice. I would get rid of it before Zack gets here. He will hurt someone." I thanked the teacher and decided to find a time to observe this group that would be promoting into my class. On Wednesday evening, I had my opportunity. Boy, was I shocked. There were 22 of them, and the room was chaos. *Where could I start?* I decided to begin teaching their class in Extended Teaching Care so that I could learn the children's names. I also thought about dividing the department into two classes, but I knew there was no room in our church for another class. We would have to make the best of the situation. In the next leadership meeting, I told my teachers that we had a challenge both in numbers and in the preschoolers' previous experience. We began to pray and plan for the group, and we contacted each parent and child.

On the first Sunday, we greeted the children. With four teachers and a department director, the group still was a challenge. When I look back, I easily recognize why we had a successful year in spite of the large group of children.

- We planned together.
- We prayed together.
- We arrived early and removed any nonessentials like extra tables, chairs, and equipment.
- All of our teachers arrived 30 minutes before the first child.
- We allowed the children to choose between at least five Bible-learning activities.
- We used natural consequences and redirection instead of "time out."
- We evaluated the session and our approaches to the children.

While I do not think things went perfectly, we did keep the blocks.

What Is Discipline?

The word *discipline* describes the process of helping a child grow as Jesus grew. In Luke 2:52, the Bible tells us that "Jesus grew in wisdom, stature, and favor with God and man." The process of developing a sense of discipline or self-control allows a child to grow in what and how he thinks, how he treats his body, and how he relates to God and people around him. Discipline should not be confused with punishment. The word *discipline* comes from the Greek word *matheteno*, which means to become a pupil or to disciple to teach. This word is positive. Punishment on the other hand is negative. These two words are not interchangeable. Consider the differences.

Discipline	Punishment
Positive	Negative
Shapes the child's future decisions	Punishes the child's past behavior
Encourages personal responsibility	Based on the expectations of the adults in charge
Seeks natural consequences	Seeks an arbitrary negative reinforcement for behavior
Encourages appropriate behavior	Discourages inappropriate behavior
Love, concern, disappointment	Tension, frustration
Child feels adult's concern	Revenge

Discipline is a system of consistent choices, consequences, and boundaries. The ultimate goal is self-discipline. In other words, when left alone a child will make right choices based on what is right, not based on the likelihood of being caught. The focus of discipline is to create an environment for the child to own his behavior and to look down the road at the consequences of his behavior. This can be accomplished by creating a track record of right choices and personal responsibility. The question every teacher should ask is not, "How can I punish this child for what he did?" but rather, "What can the child learn from this situation?"

Why do teachers avoid discipline?
• They do not know what to do.
• They have not prepared adequately for the session.
• They are too busy.
• They want the children to be happy.
• They believe giving in just once will not hurt.
• They are just trying to get through the session.
• They lack a personal relationship with the children.

To create an atmosphere of positive discipline, teachers must begin by being a positive model of a disciplined life. Preschoolers learn a great deal by example. The way a teacher treats children determines to a large degree how the children treat each other.

> Mr. Tommy says, "Inappropriate behavior that is recognized and reinforced will probably be repeated."

The Basics of Discipline

• The goal must be self-discipline.
• Maintaining the dignity of all involved is essential. Avoid yelling across the room unless a child is in danger. Communicate that the child is valued in spite of behavior rather than is worthless because of behavior. Also, be careful

of what you say to other children, parents, and teachers about a child's behavior.
- Create an environment that requires respect for self, others, and things.
- While the teacher must encourage children to take responsibility for their actions, the teacher is in charge.

What must a child believe for self-discipline to occur?
- I like the way God made me.
- I can make right decisions.
- I can think and do for myself because that is the way God made me.
- I can solve any problem with God's help.

Love the Children—Tips for Guiding Behavior

L—*Look for trouble.* The old saying "An ounce of prevention is worth a pound of cure" is true in terms of discipline. Many times teachers create a situation that tempts children toward inappropriate behavior. For example, a kickball just lying in the room for no apparent purpose tempts children to do what they know to do. Kick it. The simple solution is to remove the ball until time for outdoor play or planned use indoors.

O—*Offer appropriate choices.* Offering appropriate choices allows the child to take ownership of his behavior and allows the teacher to maintain the authority to limit the choices. The key is giving right choices.

Begin group time with a fun game that draws preschoolers into the action instead of calling the children together. If a child decides to work a puzzle, she must stick with that choice. Remind her that next week she can make a different choice. Most of the time, if teachers prepare fun games and activities for group time, preschoolers will want to be there.

> Mr. Tommy says,
> "Don't start what
> you can't finish."

V—*Value a sense of humor.* Humor is really important. The teacher must have the ability to laugh at herself. When a teacher enters the room, she must put aside personal or church problems that are currently on her mind. Humor allows the teacher to laugh with children. A teacher might say: "Did you really mean to do that?" or "There is a tricky block hiding under the shelf. Who can find it and put it back on the shelf?"

Here are a few warnings about using humor!
- Consider each child's personality.
- Avoid silly names for children.
- Humor can further deteriorate a situation if not used in a purposeful way.

E—*Encourage the child.* While this advice seems obvious to most teachers, it is frequently lost in the art of discipline. Praise must be sincere and honest. Statements like, "That is the best picture I have ever seen" are empty and probably devoid of true meaning. Words that acknowledge hard work or creativity, or phrases that are more tangible, are more meaningful to the child. Remember, praise and flattery are different. Praise should point to the positive consequences of an action: "Emil, you were very helpful in the block center. When you help in that way, we can get ready for group time very easily. Thank you."

Look for opportunities to thank a child for right choices. Many preschoolers have learned that the quickest way to get attention is to misbehave.

T—*Take time to listen.* Listen to the child's meaning as well as the child's words. Preschoolers do not have the ability to express themselves in words as fully as adults, but they do have the ability to express themselves. It is essential that we take the time to listen.

Four-year-old Sara often disrupted group time with long stories that were unrelated to the Bible story or emphasis. I suspected that Sara was trying to tell her teachers, "No one listens to me." I encouraged Sara to come to my Bible-learning center and talk all she wanted. I explained to her that during group time she should only talk when it was her turn.

Sometimes there are unspoken needs. It is difficult for a child to control his behavior if his basic needs have not been met. Lack of breakfast, a good night's sleep, or a reasonably good environment at home before the session can cause problems.

H—*Help the children understand what you want them to do.* Frequently, teachers and parents tell children what they do not want them to do, but they fail to tell them what they want them to do. For example, when children run in the hallway, most teachers say, "Don't run." Teachers should attempt to tell children what the acceptable behavior is. For instance, a teacher might say, "Walk in the hallway, please." Many children are deaf to words like *stop* and *no*. Children have heard these words too frequently so the words lose their meaning and impact. Teachers must reteach what the words mean. The words do not mean "maybe" or "if I persist." The words *no* and *stop* must be used sparingly and when there are no other options.

E—*Enable problem solving.* Learning to solve problems together is a critical skill. It not only teaches self-discipline but communication as well. Begin creating an environment for problem solving by helping children learn to use words instead of actions to communicate how they feel. Teachers must go beyond merely saying "Use your words" to modeling appropriate words. For instance, help two-year-olds learn to say, "You are in my space," rather than allowing them to bite.

Problem solving is:
  Talking to each other.
      Telling what happened.
          Telling how one feels.
              Listening to each other.
                  Planning ways to handle the situation in the future.

C—*Consider the age group.* Appropriate expectations for older preschoolers may be unrealistic for younger ages.

After a seminar on discipline and guidance, a teacher asked, "I don't understand why I can't get my 12 children to sit still for group time." When I asked about the age of the children and the number of teachers, she replied, "Oh, I teach two-year-

olds by myself." The problem was not the two-year-olds. The problem was the teacher's expectations and the child/teacher ratio. Teachers and parents should understand what is acceptable behavior and what is the normal range of parameters for each stage during the preschool years. The best way to teach Bible stories and truths to preschoolers is through activities that they enjoy and in which they can actively participate during the session. Often, teachers equate a child's capacity to sit still and listen with an ability to learn. For a two-year-old, to move is to learn. A two-year-old who is being still is probably asleep!

Another tip when considering the age group is to clarify messages. Preschoolers do not speak in adult terms, even though they may have some of an adult's vocabulary. A child's language often exceeds his understanding. When seeking to clarify messages, first get the children's attention. Say, "I need to see everyone's eyes looking at me." Understand your audience. Do not expect a three-year-old to understand or respond like a kindergartner. Using consistent wording also eliminates many misunderstandings.

H—*Have a time of renewal.* Renewal time is not a time out. "Time Out" is punishment. A renewal time is time for the child to gain control of herself. It is not punitive isolation from others or things. Renewal time can be used when a child is tired or out of control. A teacher can sit with the child until she can "control her body" or settle down. During this time, a teacher may choose to read to the child, allow him to look at a book, or draw with crayons. How long should a child remain in the renewal time? The time varies. As a rule, one minute per year of life is appropriate. Yet, a child who is tired may even need to sleep or rest, which may require 30 minutes or longer. In essence, the time should be determined by the child's response.

Some guidelines:
• Never put the child in the hall or in an area where there are no adults.
• Never put the child in a chair facing the wall or corner. This is not an impression church or teachers should leave on a child.

I—*Ignore small annoyances.* Some teachers tend to get into the "Barney Fife" mode of punishing children. This mode can be summed up in two phrases: "Nip it. Nip it in the bud." A teacher cannot catch every behavior that borders on inappropriate. In some cases, the behavior is repeated because the child has learned that the behavior gets a teacher's attention; negative attention is still attention. Some children only get a steady diet of attention through misbehavior.

L—*Look for natural and logical consequences.* The best way to teach a lesson is to make it apply. This principle is true with Bible study, math, and even discipline. Natural and logical consequences help teach lessons because they relate to the behavior.

Imagine that Emily is standing in a chair. Her teacher says: "Emily, chairs are for sitting, not standing. I am afraid you will fall and hurt yourself." This statement builds on what we know about clear messages and concern for the child. Emily folds her arms. The teacher continues: "Emily, I will not let you hurt yourself. You may either sit in the chair or stand on the floor. If you continue to stand in the chair, I will remove you and place your chair outside the room for the rest of class time." Emily continues her stance. The teacher carefully removes the child from the chair and places the chair in the closet. The teacher affirms her care for Emily, but points out that this was her choice.

D—*Direct attention to positive behavior.* Consider the children you teach. Think about a child who consistently demonstrates self-control and participation. Now, think about a child who consistently demonstrates impulsive behavior and distracts from purposeful play and teaching. Which child receives more of your attention during the session?

By recognizing positive behavior, teachers reinforce the desirable behavior. Do not say, "Adam, I like it when you keep your feet on the floor." We do not want children merely to act appropriately for our approval. We want them to choose behavior because they see the benefit for themselves and for others. Consider saying: "Thank you, Adam, for keeping your feet on the floor during the story. It helps you listen and helps others listen, too."

By directing attention to positive behavior, teachers give the child an opportunity to see what is expected. At group time, a teacher may say: "Thank you, Amanda, for looking this way while I begin my story. It helps you listen better."

R—*Reconsider the situation before acting.* Reconsider what you have said and done. Providing consistent guidelines does not mean being inflexible. Common sense is a powerful tool. Rely on it. Consider the situation in its entirety. Perhaps you only saw the last lick given or word said. Do you have enough information to intervene? Be careful not to jump to conclusions. If the children are old enough, ask questions and listen to the details. Allow the children to solve the problem themselves if possible. In some cases, the best tip is to restate the acceptable behavior and redirect the preschoolers.

E—*Enlist additional teachers.* Having the appropriate number of prepared and trained teachers is essential to teaching children and guiding behavior. There are many factors that a preschool leader cannot change, such as the size of the room or the number of children. But in every situation, the number of teachers can be adjusted. Consider adding more teachers when:
- ratios are not within acceptable ranges;
- activities, such as hammering nails into a log or cooking, require a teacher's complete attention;
- a child has a pattern of hurting himself or others; or
- a child has special needs.

Mr. Tommy says, "No technique can be effective without a strong relationship between the teacher and the child."

N—*Never give away your authority.* Sometimes it is tempting to take a child who is having difficulty controlling his actions to the parent. However, in making that choice you are telling the child and the parent that you do not possess the power to manage the situation. Cases that merit involving parents are situations that consistently endanger the child, another child, or a teacher. Avoid giving parents weekly updates on their child's behavior. If this habit is started with one child, then it sets expectations with other parents. It also puts a great deal of pressure on the parents and the child each time they come to church.

Biting is one example of a situation that needs involvement from parents. Biting is a normal reaction for children who do not have the words to adequately express their

frustration, and it is common for one-year-olds and two-year-olds. Some reasons for biting are teething, parents and siblings playing too many games with the child using their teeth, the feeling of helplessness from older siblings, or just frustration.

When a biting incident occurs, each child involved needs warm, caring attention.
1. Treat the injured child first by washing the area thoroughly with soap and water.
2. Invite the injured child to tell the other child how he feels. "You hurt me."
3. Try these following methods to deal with a biting incident:
   - In a calm but firm voice, say: "You may not bite, Andrew. Biting hurts."
   - Acknowledge the child's feelings. Comment: "You must have been very upset. Tell me why you were angry."
   - Never force the child to say, "I'm sorry."
   - Never bite the child or tell a child who was bitten to "bite back." As a teacher, you are a role model. Do not model an act of violence.
   - Inform the parents of both children in a private and confidential way.
   - Tell the parents of the injured child how you treated the bite. Avoid telling them who did the biting. This knowledge can create harsh feelings. You do not want the situation to deteriorate into a parental squabble. Explain that this behavior is normal and that occasionally all children react in physical ways. Tell them what you are doing to avoid the situation in the future.
   - When speaking with the parents of the child who bit, explain privately that this behavior is normal for one-year-olds and two-year-olds. Tell them your plans for avoiding the situation in the future. Ask for their assistance in guiding the behavior.

Develop a plan to curtail biting incidents in the future.
- Understand the reason for the incident.
- Help the child begin to use phrases with other children who are causing the frustration, such as, "You are in my space."
- Evaluate the room and the teaching plan. Do you have activities that are suitable for the children during the session? Do you have more than one of favorite items?
- Evaluate the child-teacher ratio. Are there too many children in the room? Are each child's emotional and physical needs being met? Do the children feel safe?
- With ones, you may need to enlist an extra teacher to "shadow" the child and redirect him until he works through this phase.
- Give the child a teether to use when he is frustrated.

You also have the authority to limit what type of play occurs in the room. Play that imitates violence should not be tolerated at church. If the child is using the triangle block as a gun, for instance, simply state: "We don't play or pretend that anything hurts or hits. You may choose to play something else, or you may put the block away."

When choosing a consequence, consider these questions:
* Is the consequence related to the behavior?
* Is the consequence respectful to the child?
* Is the consequence reasonable?
* Is the consequence timely?

The Room Teaches

Most preschool rooms are used by Sunday School, church weekday education, Mission Friends, choir, Discipleship Training, and child care during church events. Shared space often leads to walls and rooms that are loaded with stuff. Rooms and walls that are cluttered overstimulate and cloud the focus of the session.

The Seven Commandments of Sharing Space

1. Thou shalt remove all visuals from the walls at the end of each teaching session. Each organization should have the opportunity to use visuals on the wall that relate to the session in progress. Such visuals encourage preschoolers to focus on the Bible content of the session. Removing visuals after each session allows each preschool ministry to use the room effectively and discourages squabbles between teachers.
2. Thou shalt avoid using staples and tacks to put up visuals in preschool rooms. Bulletin boards are best used in parent areas or to display or dry the children's artwork.
3. Thou shalt paint walls with neutral colors, such as beige, off-white, or with very light pastels. Busy wallpaper, murals, or borders limit the effective use of walls in the teaching session. Overpowering colors can over-stimulate preschoolers. If murals are a "must" for your preschool building, arrange for them to be painted on large canvas panels. Mount the panels in the hallways, not in the preschool rooms. Murals often look dated very quickly and may have been given in memory of a significant person. Murals in a room can distract from the Bible story and Bible truths for the session. Teaching pictures that support the biblical emphasis are a more effective use of visuals. And larger-than-life visuals can be scary for some preschoolers.
4. Thou shalt mount teaching pictures or other visuals at the eye level of the child. Hanging things from the ceiling or high on the wall frustrates children and limits the visuals' effectiveness.
5. Thou shalt remember that less is more. The temptation for teachers is to spend a great deal of time and energy on the décor of the room. Yet preschool rooms are not living rooms. They are only a means to an end. Think of the room as a blank piece of paper each session. The true art is what happens with the child, not what is placed on the wall.
6. Thou shalt limit the equipment in the room to what is useful and suitable to the age group. When space is limited, remove tables and chairs. Avoid using chairs, including adult-sized rocking chairs, in a room for one-year-olds.
7. Thou shalt keep the room clean and remove all clutter from preschool rooms. Preschool teachers have a habit of collecting everything from old curriculum to toilet paper tubes. Preschool rooms need shelves and tubs to store resources.

Recognize that discipline matters are not a distraction from teaching biblical truths. In fact, they provide one of your greatest opportunities to apply biblical truths to a child's life in a positive way. The self-discipline a child begins to develop in your preschool class can influence every area of his life as he continues to grow physically and spiritually. Ask God for wisdom and insight as you accept this responsibility—and this privilege—each week.

Beginning Foundations: Teaching Babies and Ones

From the beginning, children are learning. What they learn depends on the kind of care and experiences they encounter early in life. Babies learn about God when they are exposed to biblical truths at home and church. In fact, God commands us to teach children, even babies, about Him as they build relationships with babies and children (Deuteronomy 6:6-7).

The recent studies on brain development are no surprise to the Great Creator. David wrote: "You created the deepest parts of my being. You put me together inside my mother's body. How you made me is amazing and wonderful. I praise you for that. What you have done is wonderful" (Psalm 139:13-14, NIrV). David recognized that only God could create something as intricate as human life.

Stages of Emotional Development

Experiences after birth determine the actual wiring of the brain.

A child learns how to relate, communicate, and think from his early interactions with others. The capacity to learn—starts in the first months of life. From birth, the baby's brain is constantly collecting information. Ninety-five percent of this information comes through his senses of seeing, hearing, and touching. As a baby takes in information through his senses, the experience is both a mental reaction as well as an emotional one. Emotional social development serves as a major building block on which the child constructs his outlook of the world. Healthy emotional development also is the building block upon which a child begins to build his understanding of the world from a biblical viewpoint and impacts how young children learn and process biblical truths.[1]

Stage 1. Develops an Awareness of His Environment (by 3 months)
During the first two or three months of life, a newborn is becoming comfortable and interested in the world around him. The infant uses his senses to take in the environment around him. He begins to achieve a sense of trust by finding familiar faces and hearing familiar voices. Through bonding with loving, nurturing adults, the baby develops trust in his environment and in the people around him. These early experiences establish important connections in the brain, the foundation for skills and traits, from self-esteem to future learning.

Stage 2. Begins to Build Relationships (by 5 months)
At two to four months, the baby becomes more emotionally responsive. The infant will coo, smile, and wiggle when she hears familiar voices. The infant becomes an active part of a loving relationship with her parents. Her interactions and relationships with significant adults will impact how she views herself and how she behaves. For example, as teachers and parents show compassion and unconditional love to her, a baby will learn to feel compassion for others. She will see herself as a person who is loved and who can give love.

Stage 3. Communicates with Others (by 9 months)

Beginning around six months of age, a baby begins to use gestures and expressions to communicate. He points or moves his arms and hands to make his desires known. He begins to realize that his actions can make things happen and can cause others to respond. When adults respond to a baby's attempts at communication, they reinforce the child's efforts. He continues to gesture and communicate. Encourage communication with interactive games, such as peekaboo. Notice the facial expressions babies make when expressing joy, surprise, or frustration. Mirror these sounds and expressions back to them playfully.

Stage 4. Develops Sense of Who He Is (by 14 to 18 months)

A child's picture of himself becomes clearer through communication. His sense of self grows through imitating the motions, gestures, expressions, and tones of voices of the people he loves. As a child imitates others, he shows that he has made a connection between what he sees and hears and what he does. Concepts of caring and compassion are conveyed as adults encourage a child to gently hold and rock a doll. Looking at the Bible and linking conversation about God and Jesus to his experiences lays the foundation for a child to become aware that God made him and that he is a special and unique person.

Stage 5. Develops New Ideas (by 24 to 30 months)

The child has the ability to think, solve problems, and express emotions using words. The child in this stage sees a problem, creates a solution, and tries it out. A child can look at the Bible and figure out how to open it and turn the pages. As she moves about and interacts with the environment, she gains more information. Movement integrates and anchors information and experience in the brain.

Teaching Biblical Truths

The first step in teaching biblical truths is to be sure the physical environment is safe and sanitary. Clean cribs, toys, and teaching materials with a bleach and water solution. Parents will feel more comfortable about bringing their young child to church if they know the environment is clean and safe.

Through Relationships

Hold, hug, and rock infants. The way you hold an infant impacts his sense of trust and security. The feel of a warm body, loving arms, and a steady heartbeat brings a feeling of warmth and security. Most babies are soothed by rocking and gentle side-to-side movements. Try swaying slowly, taking four to five seconds to move from one side to the other. Vary the positions to see which positions allow his muscles to relax. Your gentle touch may soothe and comfort infants.

However, keep in mind that the touch that may delight some babies but may feel irritating to others.

As you hold and rock, look into the baby's eyes and talk about God and Jesus. Use simple Bible phrases or Bible story conversation. At birth, a baby's sense of hearing is better developed than his ability to see. Babies enjoy the different pitches and rhythms of the human voice. Talk to young infants as you change a diaper, give a bottle, or shake a rattle. Relate the experience to God by saying: "Thank You, God, for milk. God gives Jasmine milk."

With ones and twos, teachers can continue to build upon relationships. Listen as a ones babbles to you. When he pauses, talk to him. Pause and allow him to respond. Listen as older ones and twos talk. Respond warmly as a child hugs you.

Through Music

> American Academy of Pediatrics recommends that healthy babies sleep on their backs. Be sure to check with parents about their babies sleep position.

Babies are soothed by the beat, rhythms, and repetitive patterns found in music. Sing simple words to familiar tunes to soothe and comfort a fussy infant. Play a recording of instrumental hymns as soft background music. Hum quietly as you rock a tired baby. When a child arrives, to the tune "London Bridge" sing: "I am glad to see my friend, see my friend, see my friend. I am glad to see my friend. Jordan came to church." Clap an older babies hands together as you sing a clapping song. Hang wind chimes and as the chimes ring, say: "We can hear the chimes. Thank You, God, for ears to hear." Encourage ones and twos to shake homemade shakers while you sing. Sing a Bible phrase as children play.

Homemade Wind Chimes—Cut a cardboard strip 1½ to 2 inches wide and about 9 inches long. (These measurements are approximate. You can adjust as desired.) Hold the cardboard strip lengthwise and punch a hole in each of the upper corners of the cardboard. Cut an 18-inch length of fishing line. Tie one end of the line through one hole and one end of the line through the other hole. Punch holes along the bottom of the cardboard (as many as desired). Tie a 10-inch length of fishing line through each hole. At the other end of each line, securely tie a large screw, key, spoon, or other chiming item. Use another piece of fishing line to hang the chimes from the ceiling.

Through Mobiles

> Repetition of activities is needed to firm up connections in the brain. When a connection is used repeatedly in the early years, it becomes permanent.

Suspend items from the ceiling. As you hold a baby, look at the interesting items and talk about them. Hang a picture of Jesus at shoulder level. Say: "I see a picture of Jesus. Jesus loves you." Suspend a gift bag from the ceiling, low enough for you to reach inside it. Place a toy or other item inside the bag. Tape a small picture to the outside of the bag. Hold a baby so she can see the picture; talk about the picture. Reach inside the bag and take out the toy. Hang a variety of items such as beach balls, colorful ribbons, wind chimes, and nature items. The children will enjoy seeing the different items, touching them, and making them move.

Streamer Mobile—Cut eight different colored ribbons. The ribbon pieces do not need to all be the same length. Tie the end of each piece of ribbon to an embroidery hoop. Space the ribbons evenly around the hoop. Use yarn to hang the hoop from the ceiling.

Through Toys

Provide appropriate toys and teaching materials. Toys, books, and pictures provide opportunities for teachers to relate Bible phrases, Bible story conversation, and Bible stories to babies and young preschoolers.

Guidelines for Choosing Toys at Church
- Easy to clean and disinfect
- Suitable for the age and developmental needs of the children
- Free of cartoon and fantasy characters
- Actively involves children in doing and thinking
- Free of small parts. Test the size of toys with a choke-tube made with a toilet tissue tube. If the toy passes through the tube, it is too small to be used with preschoolers.

The chart on page 55 lists appropriate toys for babies, ones, and twos.

Teacher-made Toys
Often babies, ones, and twos enjoy teacher-made toys. When making toys, remember:
1. Make them appealing.
2. Make them durable.
3. Make them safe.

Tips for Making Toys
- Infants and young preschoolers prefer primary colors and geometric shapes.
- Make openings clearly visible by placing brightly-colored tape around the edges.
- Reinforce the corners and edges of boxes and lids with plastic tape.
- Create smooth, round edges.
- Cut strings or ribbons less than 12 inches long.
- Eliminate small parts that a child could swallow.

Viewing Bottle—Add pieces of curly gift ribbon, metallic garland, colorful tissue paper, shaped metallic confetti, or other colorful items in a small clear plastic bottle or water bottle. Seal the lid with glue and wide transparent tape. Shake the bottle or roll it to a baby or one-year-old. (Other ideas: add plastic spools, colored rice, or candy sprinkles; use two-liter bottles and nature items.)

Through Books
Books can help teachers communicate Bible truths to babies, ones, and twos. Place a book in a baby's bed. As the baby grasps the book, say: "You see a book about Jesus." Lay a book on the floor near a toy. Encourage a child to turn the book pages while she sits near you. Keep a book near a rocking chair. Read the book as you comfort a baby. All the books you provide should support the Bible truth that you are teaching. Choose books that are durable and washable. Books should have colorful, realistic pictures and few or no words.

See Chapter 17 for more information on making toys for preschoolers.

Photo Album Book—Take photos of the younger preschoolers in your department/class. Place the photos in a small, self-adhesive photo album. Encourage children to turn the pages and look at pictures of friends.

The most important book is the Bible. Place the Bible on the floor for younger preschoolers to touch and see. Turn the pages of the Bible as you say, "Thank You, God, for the Bible." As a child looks at a picture in the Bible, use conversation about the Bible story. Place a paper strip in the Bible at the reference for a Bible phrase. Older ones and twos can take the strip out of the Bible or turn Bible pages to find the strip. Read the Bible phrase. As a child carries the Bible, say, "We learn about the Bible at church."

Through Nature Items
Safe nature items encourage younger preschoolers to use their senses. They can smell an orange, feel a feather, see a colorful flower, taste applesauce, and hear rocks fall into a

can. Use these opportunities to teach preschoolers about God through His creation.
- Place nature items in a clear jar for children to see and handle.
- Provide some items for children to touch with your supervision.
- Place a small amount of water in a dishpan for babies or younger ones to splash. Older ones and twos can pour the water using plastic cups.
- Watch a goldfish swimming in a plastic bottle.
- Walk outside in a safe area and observe God's creation.

Color Bottle—Fill a clear plastic bottle halfway with water. Add blue food color until the water is light to medium blue. Add enough mineral oil so that it is about one inch above the water line. (Baby oil may be used.) Seal the lid with glue and wide transparent tape.

Through Pictures

Teaching pictures can provide opportunities to talk about Bible truths. Cover pictures with clear contact plastic (or protect them in another way) so younger preschoolers can safely handle them without damaging them. To make them more durable, mount them on cardboard before covering them. Simple pictures without a lot of detail allow babies to focus on the main subject of a picture. Place pictures in baby beds and on the floor. Tape a small picture to the back of a rocking chair so a baby can see it when you hold him on your shoulder. Place small pictures in the Bible for preschoolers to find.

Picture Flaps—Place self-adhesive notes on sections of a teaching picture. You may put a note over a face or other significant item. Encourage a child to lift the "flap" to see what's underneath the note. Say: "I see Jesus' face. Jesus loves you.".

Through Puzzles and Manipulatives

Children enjoy toys that involve pulling apart and putting together. Fill-and-dump toys, nesting toys, and stacking toys are all types of manipulative toys for babies and ones. Older ones and twos also use wooden puzzles. As a child pulls apart pop beads, say: "Look what you can do! Thank You, God, for Crystal's hands." Use puzzles to relate the child's actions to the Bible truth. Children can begin to learn that the Bible is a book for them.

Clothespin Drop—Cover the sides of a two-pound coffee can with colorful contact plastic. Cut an X in the plastic lid with a utility knife. Add eight peg-type clothespins to the can. Invite younger preschoolers to push the clothespins through the slits in the lid. Remove the lid and guide younger preschoolers to drop the clothespins in the can and pour them out. Older ones and twos will enjoy slipping the clothespins onto the rim of the can.

Through Blocks

Provide homemade or purchased cardboard and plastic blocks for younger preschoolers to use. Place a block on top of a large mat. Place a toy on one side of the block. Encourage the baby to crawl over or around the block to get the toy. As ones stack the blocks, say: "We can work together with our friends. Thank You, God, for friends." Allow preschoolers to knock down their block stacks. Place a large paper sack in the block area so ones and twos can fill and empty it with blocks. Offer cars and trucks or plastic animal figures for preschoolers to use. Use items that lead to talking about the Bible truths.

For more information about teaching Bible truths using Bible-learning centers and activities, see Chapters 8-14.

Milk-carton Blocks—For each block, you will need two milk cartons of the same size. Cut the top away from each carton. Stuff one carton tightly with crushed newspaper. With the open ends together, push one carton inside the other. Secure the cartons with masking tape. Cover the block with contact plastic. Make several different sizes.

Through Homeliving Materials

Toys that remind children of everyday experiences help them feel more secure at church. Toy telephones, dolls and blankets, plastic dishes, and other homeliving items can all be used to teach Bible truths. Place a mirror in a baby bed. Say, "Thank You, God, for Abby," as she looks in the mirror. Attach a full-length unbreakable mirror to the wall horizontally for babies to see themselves as they crawl. A vertical full-length mirror attached to the wall can be used with ones and twos. Wrap a doll in a blanket and place it on the floor. Say: "You can help take care of the doll. Mommy takes care of you. Thank You, God, for Mommy." Place plastic dishes on the floor for twos to have a pretend picnic. Say, "In the Bible, we read 'God gives food to us.' "

Food Boxes—Stuff small empty food boxes with newspaper. Choose food boxes that may be familiar to younger preschoolers (cereal boxes, cracker boxes, and so forth). Tape the boxes closed with transparent tape. Provide a paper bag with the food boxes. As the children play with the boxes and bag, say, "God gives food to us."

Through Art Materials

Older ones and twos can use simple art materials to express themselves. These creative experiences can be used to teach Bible truths. Provide large crayons and paper for older ones and twos. Tape a piece of contact plastic to the wall, sticky side out; add a basket of felt or fabric shapes for younger preschoolers to stick to the contact plastic. Twos will enjoy painting on cafeteria trays or an easel. As children work, say: "You are growing. You can do many things. The Bible says, 'God made me.' "

Chunk Crayons—Place foil liners in muffin pan cups. Drop small pieces of broken crayons into each section of the pan. (Separate the crayons by color and remove the paper.) Place the pan in a warm oven (200 to 250 degrees) until the crayon bits are completely melted. Stir the melted crayons occasionally with a wooden craft stick. Remove the pan from the oven. When the crayons are completely cooled, remove the foil liners. Older ones and twos can use these chunk crayons with paper to create designs.

> A baby needs to know he is deeply and consistently loved. He will flourish when someone responds to his sounds of frustration or pleasure.

Use this checklist to determine if you are teaching Bible truths to babies in your church.

____Teachers encourage babies to touch and hold the Bible as they talk about God and Jesus.
____Teachers talk about the Bible as they use pictures, books, and toys.
____Teachers sing and talk to babies as they meet basic needs of diapering, feeding, and holding.
____Teachers build relationships and trust with babies by committing to teach every week rather than on a rotating basis.
____Teachers use Bible phrases, Bible story conversation, and songs to encourage Bible learning on the child's level of understanding.
____Teachers are trained in the use of curriculum and are equipped with an understanding of the importance of Bible teaching for young preschoolers.

Help for Common Situations

Comforting a Distressed Infant

Prolonged crying is stressful to both adult and baby. Sometimes it even appears contagious. During the first few months of life, teachers should not let a baby cry indefinitely. Babies at this stage cannot be spoiled by adults who are attentive to their needs. Try these techniques for infants under 12 months.

- Put a peaceful expression on your face.
- Remain calm. Speak in a soothing tone of voice.
- Hold and look into his face from a distance neither too close nor too far.
- Gently rock the infant in a rocking chair.
- Place a music box in the baby's crib or play soft background music.
- Rub the baby's back, using a small circular motion.
- Lay the infant on her back and gently stroke her forehead and cheeks.
- Provide a distraction such as a plastic rattle or a colorful block. Talk softly as you engage the infant in playing with the toy.

Separation Anxiety

Separation anxiety is a normal and important step in an infant's emotional development. Separation anxiety is an increased unwillingness to be separated from his primary caregiver, usually his mother. Around 7 months, separation anxiety peaks, and the infant discovers that when a parent is out of sight. This separation is a primary cause of emotional stress for a baby. Because a baby has no sense of time, every separation seems too long. The separation process is even more unpleasant if the baby is tired or hungry.

Tips for Dealing with Separation Anxiety
1. Greet the child and parents at the door.
2. For preschoolers who are walking, ask parents to allow their child to knock on the door and walk into the room.
3. Create a distraction as the parent leaves. (Show the child a picture or sing a song.)
4. Tell the parents to say good-bye.
5. Reassure the child that Mommy and Daddy will be back.
6. Continue to hold the child until you believe she will be comfortable on the floor or in a crib. At this point, another teacher may need to take information from the parents.
7. Maintain eye contact and speak softly.

Babies, ones, and twos need a safe, loving environment that stimulates them to explore, manipulate, wonder, and discover God's world. They need teachers who engage in conversation about God, Jesus, and the Bible and teachers who are aware that they are the example of God's unconditional love to the children they teach. As a teacher, you are living the lesson of God's love to the children entrusted to your care. Babies can learn. Babies can learn about God. What lessons are you teaching?

[1] Adapted from Stanley Greenspan in *Building Healthy Minds* (Cambridge, MA: Perseus Books, 1999).

Toys and Manipulatives

Age

Toys and Manipulatives

Birth—3 months

Easy-to-grasp rattles
Mobiles with pieces that hang horizontally
Pictures and toys with bold black, white, and red designs
Musical toys, soft background music

3—6 months

Rattles
Plastic rings
Large plastic beads
Measuring cups
Plastic containers
Textured balls
Unbreakable crib mirror
Crib activity centers
Musical toys, soft background music

9—12 months

Pull-and-push toys
Fill-and-dump toys
Balls
Crib activity centers
Stacking and nesting toys
Textured balls and toys

12—18 months

Toy telephone
Musical toys
Sturdy cars and trucks
Pop-up toys
Hammering/pounding toys
Cardboard blocks
Nesting/stacking toys
Child-sized rocker

18—24 months

Push-and-pull toys
Simple puzzles with whole pieces
Nesting toys
Shape sorters
Toy telephones
Homeliving props (plastic dishes but no forks and knifes)
Dolls

Making Transitions: Teaching Kindergartners

Chapter 7

The term *kindergarten* is used today to define or describe the five- and six-year-old's entrance into formal schooling. In most school settings, kindergarten is viewed as a transition time between preschool and the more formal education of first grade. Much of the same philosophy holds true for the kindergarten classroom in church settings.

Kindergartners are . . .

The kindergarten year is a period of slow growth. Traditionally, the kindergartner grows taller, and her hands and feet grow larger. The kindergartner laughs and cries easily and is prone to self-criticism. In addition, the kindergartner:
- exhibits more controlled behavior, replacing earlier exuberant behaviors.
- is competent, reliable, and takes responsibilities seriously.
- has greater fine muscle control, enabling more controlled, precise movement.
- uses a vocabulary of thousands of words.
- enjoys social activities that revolve around special friendships.
- participates in more involved and imaginative group play.

Kindergartners need . . .

- opportunities for expressive activities such as those available through dramatic play.
- opportunities to use imaginative and creative talents
- time to talk, observe, discover, and experiment.
- a calm, stress-free, stimulating, challenging, and secure environment.
- problem-solving and choice-making situations appropriate for their level of understanding.
- caring, nurturing adults.
- opportunities to explore their world in depth and assimilate what they learn through multiple experiences.
- ways to investigate and find answers to questions and then express those answers in a variety of formats. such as drawing, painting, and building with blocks or play dough.

Even though kindergartners have a growing knowledge of reading and writing, they still learn best through multiple experiences. Multiple experiences are best provided through the use of Bible-learning centers such as creative art, manipulatives and puzzles, dramatic play, nature and science, music, books, and blocks and construction. The center approach allows kindergartners to engage in hands-on discovery and problem-solving and recognizes that kindergartners are developing physically, socially/emotionally, mentally, and spiritually.

Reading and Writing

When describing the skills of kindergartners, many teachers think of the children's growing knowledge of reading and writing. Often this process is referred to as *emergent literacy*. Kindergartners begin to understand the concepts of reading and writing as they experience supportive print-rich environments. What a blessing it is to a child's life when the words *church*, *God*, and *Jesus* are some of the first words he reads and when the Bible is one of the first books from which he reads! Teachers at church have a wonderful opportunity to take advantage of each child's natural curiosity by teaching biblical truths.

Learning to Write

Learning to write is a process that begins as preschoolers become aware of the differences between drawing and writing. Around age three, children begin creating a series of wavy, circular, or vertical lines called mock writing. By age five, mock writing is replaced by a mixture of letters and innovative symbols. When preschoolers start to recognize letters of the alphabet, they spell by finding the sound that most closely fits what they want to write. They often may use only the beginning letter to represent a word.[1] The early writings of children will contain backward letters and writing all over the page. Kindergartners also will hold their pencils in many different ways. Each child must develop the correct muscles to hold a pencil the "right way." Some kindergartners may hold the pencils with their fists, while others may be more comfortable with other grips. Holding a pencil is a skill that develops with practice in writing. Correct spelling should be a minor issue in kindergarten. Teachers need to create a supportive environment where children feel at ease trying out different ideas about reading and writing. An overemphasis on correctly spelling words often makes kindergartners stop trying to spell. As their knowledge and understanding of the printed word grows, they naturally begin to spell words correctly.

Stages of Writing
* scribbling (making marks)
* mock writing (letter-like forms)
* inventive spelling (words that are written according to sound)
* conventional spelling (words spelled correctly)

Using Reading and Writing to Teach Bible Truths

1. Take advantage of each child's desire to read and write.
Kindergartners are interested in reading and writing. Teachers can support kindergartners' beginning efforts by providing suitable materials. Consider making these kinds of materials available in your classroom.
• Magnetic letters and numbers (Create your own magnetic letters by attaching small magnets to the back of preprinted manuscript letters and numbers.)
• Letter tiles such as those found in Scrabble® games
• Dry erase marker boards and toxic-free dry erase markers designed for children, small chalkboards, and erasable slates

2. Provide a print-rich environment.

- Print Bible phrases or verses on sentence strips for boys and girls to see. When using Bible phrases in conversation, point to the words as you read them.
- Point to simple words such as *God, Jesus, church,* and *love* in the Bible. Invite a child to read the words.
- Label a few objects in the room, such as the Bible, doors, and stove. Print words on sentence strips or index cards using upper and lowercase manuscript letters. As kindergartners see words, they will become more familiar with them.
- Create a "Word Bank." Locate a box with a lid. Gather pictures of single items such as a Bible, a church, a teacher, and Jesus. Glue each picture onto a piece of heavyweight paper. Beneath the picture, print the name of the item. Place the cards in the word bank for preschoolers to enjoy.

3. Read and discuss books and stories.

Children understand stories better when they have opportunities to ask and answer questions about the story's characters and relate the story to their own lives. Recent research on brain development supports the importance of offering children opportunities to give feedback on concepts and ideas they are experiencing. Remember that much of what kindergartners learn cannot be processed consciously because it happens too fast. Kindergartners need time to process information.

4. Provide story-reading experiences.

To acquire a sense of what a story is and how it is organized, kindergartners need to have exposure to a story in a variety of ways. For example, knowing how a story begins and ends and the story's sequence of events is important (beginning, middle, end). Use a Bible story several times during a session in a variety of ways (recorded, seeing in print, telling, playing out). Using different methods helps the children to identify the beginning, middle, and end of the story. Retell part of the Bible story and let kindergartners tell whether the part is from the beginning, middle, or end of the Bible story.

5. Read books more than once.

Children are more likely to reenact or role-play a book or story on their own if they have heard it at least three times. When reading a book to children, stop occasionally and ask them to predict what will happen next. Encouraging more than one response helps children begin to understand that there is more than one answer to a problem. Asking them to consider other possibilities helps children think and formulate new ideas.

6. Link reading and writing to Bible-learning center activities.

Include paper, pencils, and felt-tip markers in learning centers to encourage the use of writing and reading as children play. A notepad in the dramatic play center may be used to print a grocery list or letter. Index cards in the block center can be used to create traffic signs or label structures.

Kindergartners and Computers

Many kindergartners are expert computer users. Using computers with kindergartners, especially at church, raises some questions.

Why do kindergartners like computers?
Kindergartners have a strong need to make things happen. Computer games and activities give children a sense of control. The computer allows children to experiment and repeat the same activity over and over again.

What guidelines should teachers keep in mind when using computers with children?
- *Encourage cooperative play rather than solitary play.* Most children prefer playing on the computer with other children or adults rather than alone. Children often seek help or initiate interactions with others while involved in computer activities.
- *Choose software that includes open-ended activities.* Open-ended programs allow kindergartners to explore a concept without fear of making a mistake.
- *Offer computer programs designed to be used by several people at a time.* These programs ensure that children do not have long periods of isolation while using a computer.
- *Remember that computer Bible games only lead children to acquire facts.* They do not lead preschoolers to apply the Bible to their lives. Kindergartners still learn best about God's world by experiencing it firsthand.

Activity Ideas for Kindergarten Classrooms

1. Written (Print) Letters
- Letter cards—Write letters on index cards.
- One-inch ceramic letter tiles—Purchase blank tiles from a craft or home supply store. Use a permanent marker or paint pen to write letters on the tiles. Make sets of both uppercase and lowercase letters.
- Velcro letters—Print letters on small index cards and back them with strips of Velcro.
- Craft stick letters—Print letters on craft sticks and place them in a container for kindergartners to use to spell words.

2. Name Cards
Write each child's name on an index card. Glue his picture to the card and cover it with clear contact plastic.

3. Word Window
Cut a rectangular hole in the center of a sentence strip or strip of construction paper. Kindergartners can use the "window" to find words in a Bible phrase. Post-it® Tape Flags also may be used to highlight words in a Bible phrase or Bible story.

4. Sentence Cubes
Cover boxes of different sizes with contact plastic, making sure you have a box for each word in a sentence or Bible phrase. Print the words on index cards or pieces of construction paper and tape to the boxes. Guide kindergartners to place the boxes in the correct order. Tip: If a permanent marker is used—you can write on contact plastic and remove with hair spray.

5. Word Slides

To make a word slide, fold the top and bottom edges of a piece of cardboard or construction paper. Write a Bible phrase or statement on a sentence strip. Read the Bible phrase to the children and then place the word slide over one of the words in the sentence. Read the sentence again, skipping the hidden word. Slowly reveal the word by moving the word slide and uncovering the first letter. Ask the children to guess the word. Continue uncovering the letters of the word until they guess the word.

6. Graphs and Charts

Graphing and charting activities promote problem-solving skills in young children. As kindergartners gather and record information and interpret graphs, they acquire important mathematical skills such as number recognition, counting, and comparing. Graphing and charting activities lead kindergartners to experience the awe and wonder of God's world.

Graphing activities for kindergartners should begin with graphs which use real objects. Move to picture graphs which use pictures or models to represent objects. Begin graphing activities with two-column graphs and gradually progress to three and four columns.

Construct a large floor graph with laminated mural paper, an old shower curtain, window shade, or bed sheet. Use colored plastic tape or a permanent marker to form the grid. These grids are good for sorting and graphing large objects such as shoes and food items. Make smaller grids from shoe box lids, egg cartons, muffin pans, and ice cube trays. Use the small grids for items such as candies, blocks, or crayons.

Activities with Bible Phrases

1. **Newspaper Hunt**—Give kindergartners a word from a Bible phrase and a page from a newspaper. Guide them to circle the letters and draw a line connecting each letter until they have formed the word.
2. **Write the Verse**—Print Bible phrases or words that relate to the session on strips of paper. Provide clipboards, paper, and pencils for kindergartners to copy the words. Ask children to read what they wrote to each other or to a teacher.
3. **Match Bible Phrases**—Glue two clothespins onto a large craft stick. Write Bible phrases on index cards, one per card. Draw or glue an appropriate picture on the back of each card. Cut the cards in half. Scramble the cards and guide kindergartners to match the pictures, clip them to the clothespins, and turn over the craft stick to discover the Bible phrase printed on the back of the card.
4. **Match Bible Phrase Words**—Print a Bible phrase on a sentence strip or long strip of paper. Cut apart the phrase and give a word to each child. Provide magnetic letters (or letter tiles) and ask each kindergartner to spell his word. Put the magnetic words together to spell the Bible phrase. Read the phrase together.

[1] Eva Essa, *Introduction to Early Childhood Education* (Albany, Delmar Publishers, 1996), 362.

Creating Art

As Kendall and Joshua painted with watercolors, Kendall exclaimed, "Look Joshua, I made purple!" Kendall and Joshua are young artists at work. They are busy discovering the nature of their world. They are at play. Young children enjoy manipulating materials they find around them to express their feelings and what they know about their world. Young children are not conscious artists in the way adults are. They are not creating a product; they are involved in a process of discovery. Doing, exploring, creating, and experimenting are more important than the end result. Often the process ends in a smear of paint on paper. However, if the children have tried something new, learned something interesting, discovered characteristics of paint, or experienced the awe of God's world, they have had a successful art experience. In the art process, each child needs only to please himself and have freedom to create, discover, drip, smudge, glop, and sculpt. Because preschoolers do not yet have skillful control over the materials, they will make messes. Sometimes young children glue paper to the table or spill paint on their shoes, but they are still creating and learning.

Values

Physical

- Provides experience and practice in developing and refining gross motor or large muscle skills
- Provides movements for hand and finger muscles that are developing toward properly holding and using a pencil

Mental

- Allows opportunities for making choices
- Helps children learn about the concepts of color, shape, size, and texture
- Enhances thinking skills as children translate ideas, concepts, and experiences into art
- Allows children to practice problem-solving and reasoning skills
- Strengthens each child's imagination and creativity

Social/Emotional

- Provides pleasurable experiences for children
- Gives each child his first opportunity to put thoughts and emotions on paper
- Allows children to nonverbally express ideas, objects, experiences, and events that are emotionally significant
- Enhances children's self-confidence
- Allows children to work together, take turns, and share materials
- Teaches responsibility for cleanup and return of materials

Spiritual

- Allows children to express their ideas about God
- Creates opportunities for children to express biblical truths
- Provides opportunities for teachers to use meaningful and appropriate conversation about God, Jesus, and the Bible
- Helps children experience a sense of awe regarding God's world

Stages of Art

The Basic Scribbles

Single curved line

Multiple vertical line

Multiple diagonal line

Spiral line

Multiple loop line

Children's art moves in a predictable sequence of development. As babies and ones develop physically, they gain more control of their arms. By 18 months, children usually have gained enough control that they can make sweeping arcs with crayons or paint. At 2½ years of age, children have wrist control and begin to make circular motions in their scribbles. As children gain greater control of their movements, their art includes broad strokes, curves, ovals, and spirals, and the lines begin to run in horizontal or diagonal directions.

By three or four years of age, children gain more control of their smaller hand muscles, and their drawings become more complex. Circles become mandalas or radials. A mandala is a circle with lines that divide it into sections. Many of the drawings resemble suns. Because children like the circles they are able to draw, they decorate them with lines, crosses, and other marks. At 5 or 5½ years of age, control moves from the wrist to the fingertips. Children have full control over the entire hand. Along with the development of arm and hand movements, children are learning to control the movements of other parts of the body. Children learn that things move toward them and away from them. They learn concepts of up and down in relation to their bodies and then to other objects.

Understanding these stages of art is important when planning art experiences for young children. This information helps teachers not expect too much from young children and helps parents understand that their children are "normal" when they only scribble on the page.

Diagram Shapes

Design Shapes

Pictorial Stage

After examining children's drawings from all over the world, Rhoda Kellogg discovered that all children progress through the same stages of art. Her extensive observation resulted in the identification of four stages of art development.
Stage 1: Basic Scribbles—Twenty kinds of markings are evident in the scribblings of children two and younger. These basic scribbles are the building blocks of art.
Stage 2: Diagram Shapes—Ovals, triangles, rectangles, squares, and diagonal crosses appear in the art of three-year-olds. These diagrams represent each child's increasing ability to make controlled use of lines in the scribbling stage.
Stage 3: Design Stage—When children begin to combine diagrams or shapes, they enter the design stage. Mandalas, suns, and radials appear in the art of three- and four-year-olds.
Stage 4: Pictorial Stage—Designs combine to suggest pictures of humans, animals, buildings, vegetation, and transportation. Five-year-olds in this stage focus on drawings of the human figure, usually themselves or family members.

The Art Center

Keep a well-stocked art box accessible for children in the art center. Include a variety of paper, crayons, washable markers, scissors, and glue. From time to time, place a "surprise" in the art box, such as colored chalk, clear adhesive tape, or stickers. Other guidelines include:

- Locate the center near a water source. If the center cannot be near a sink or restroom, provide a dishpan with a small amount of soap and water for cleanup.
- Provide a safe place for drying paintings.
- Protect surfaces of tables with plastic or vinyl tablecloths, newspaper, or large pieces of paper. Use drop cloths, large vinyl tablecloths, or shower curtain liners under easels or on the floor during messy activities.
- Provide painting smocks to protect children's clothing. Purchase painting smocks or use adult blouses or shirts worn backward with the sleeves cut off. Small adult shirts are another option.

Basic Art Supplies

art tissue paper	large rolls of white or colored paper
cardboard	coffee filters
chalk (colored, white)	craft sticks
crayons	fabric scraps
felt-tip washable markers	flour
food color	nontoxic school glue
hole punch	masking tape
matte board	sponges
paintbrushes	blunt-tipped scissors
starch (liquid)	washable tempera paint
watercolor	wood scraps
yarn	

paper (construction paper, manila paper, newsprint, finger paint paper)
collage items (pictures, nature items, fabric)

Role of the Teacher

Teachers provide indirect guidance through planning and placement of the materials. As children enjoy the art materials, teachers can relate biblical truths, tell portions of a Bible story, and incorporate Bible phrases. By setting guidelines, the teacher is free to help children make the fullest use of art materials. Children need to know that they are free to make choices.

Guidelines for Children

1. Handle art tools carefully.
2. Art materials are for creating.
3. Use art materials as needed, not in a wasteful manner.
4. Glue, paint, chalk, or any other art materials are not to be put in children's mouths.
5. Keep art materials in the art center.
6. Avoid interfering with the work of other children.

Guidance Tips for Teachers

1. Avoid models for children to copy and avoid coloring book drawings. These limit a child's creativity.
2. Emphasize the creative process, not the product or end result. Avoid asking, "What's this?" when referring to a piece of artwork. Children should be free to create with the materials. This question places too much emphasis on a product. Instead, ask the child about the picture. Make comments such as "You did a good job" quietly to the child.
3. Allow messes. Creative art is messy. That is one reason children enjoy it.
4. Give children plenty of time for art activities. The process of creating often takes time and thought.
5. Involve children in cleanup. They can learn from washing paintbrushes, sponging off easels, and wiping up spills.
6. Try an art activity before using it with children. Paint consistency, paper size, or other potential problems can be solved if you take the time to pretest the project.
7. Respect each child's name. Ask the child where he would like his name printed on the paper or allow the child to print his own name.
8. Once the materials are prepared, allow the children to do the work themselves without your direct assistance. Encourage them to explore, experiment, and discover.
9. Help the children understand that they only need to please themselves with what they create.
10. Teach parents about the process of creative art. Help them understand that the purpose of children's art is not to make something to take home but to provide opportunities for teaching biblical truths and for developing creative skills.

> "Children should leave with love in their hearts, knowledge in their heads, but not necessarily something in their hands." Alma May Scarborough

Kinds of Art Experiences

Too many activities masquerade as creative art. Activities such as coloring sheets, tracing patterns, dot-to-dot sheets, holiday gifts, and crafts are labeled as art. Yet, these activities do not allow for creativity. Activities that masquerade as creative art:
- emphasize teacher input,
- have a high degree of structure, and
- result in a product where every child's looks alike.

The following ideas are examples of creative art. These activities allow preschoolers to choose what to create and allow them to express their own ideas and feelings.

> Merely labeling an activity "art" is no guarantee the activity has artistic value.

Painting

Tempera paint is the most satisfactory paint for general use. Buy well-known brands. Good tempera paint is nontoxic, bright and clear, washable, and creamy. Look for paint in nonbreakable containers that pour easily. Vary the density by the amount of water or other liquid you add. Tip: Add 1 part water, 2 parts powdered tempera, and a drop or two of liquid soap.

Clear plastic containers that let the paint color show through are the best containers for paint. These are available from educational supply companies. Empty food cans also make good paint containers. Six-ounce tomato paste cans are excellent for two- and three-year-olds. Paint the cans to match the color of paint you will put in them.
Mix tempera paint with one of the following ingredients:
- white glue for shiny paint
- liquid starch for smooth paint

- cornstarch for hard, porcelain-type quality paint
- paste for thick, textured frosting-like paint
- whipped soap flakes or granules for very thick painting
- shampoo for fluffy, whipped paint

Spread very thick paint with craft sticks or spoons. Remember that paint mixed with different ingredients allows children opportunities for discovery. You can also mix liquid hand soap with paint for easier cleanup of hands and clothes.

Dipping Art—Fold absorbent paper towels or coffee filters into four parts. Dip each corner into a container of thin paint. Unfold the towel to reveal unique designs of color. *Variation:* Cut holes in each corner of the towel before dipping it.

Negative Space Painting—Make negative space paper by cutting small shapes in a larger piece of paper. Painting becomes a problem-solving opportunity as the children decide how to utilize the holes.

Collage/Paper

Collage-making gives children the opportunity to arrange paper and materials on a flat surface such as a piece of cardboard, paper, or contact paper. Collages are made from all kinds of pieces of paper, scraps of cloth, wood, cardboard, and buttons.

Paper Collage—Scraps of construction paper are a good medium for beginning collages. Cut the scraps to workable sizes. Provide a variety of colors, shapes, and sizes. Place the scraps in a plastic shoe box.
Variations:
- Shape collage—Put paper or material into various shapes and glue to paper.
- Art collage—Provide a variety of media such as felt, burlap, tissue, yarn, and ribbon for children to glue to paper.
- Gift wrap paper—Cut shapes from different kinds of gift wrap paper (no fantasy themes).
- Nature collage—Glue items found on a nature walk onto paper or a wooden shingle.
- Tissue paper—Tear or cut into a variety of shapes.

Chalk

Painting Ideas—1. Cover paper with liquid starch and draw on it with chalk.
2. Soak chalk in water and draw on paper.
3. Cover paper with a wash of white tempera.
4. Draw with colored chalk.

Crayons and Markers

Wet Markers—Draw with markers. Use a wet brush to paint over the pictures. The colors will mix and run. *Hint:* Use the wet brush frequently. The colors mix and run better if the ink is not completely dry.

Scissors—Learning to use scissors is one of the important achievements of early childhood. Children discover that scissors give them the power to make changes in paper and other materials. Cutting looks easy, but tiny immature finger muscles are not easily directed to move in the manner to control the opening and closing of scissors.

For beginners, blunt-tipped scissors or safety scissors made of plastic with metal inserts

work well. These scissors cut art materials, not fingers. As children grow, they advance to scissors with stainless steel blades. Almost all scissors on the market today come with plastic handles and are designed to work for both right- and left-handed cutting. Snip-loop scissors are made with a looped handle so children with special needs can easily manipulate them by squeezing and releasing the loop.

Safety Limits for Using Scissors (ages three through kindergarten)
1. Scissors may be used only at the table.
2. Give scissors to another person with the handle toward him and the pointed end toward you.
3. Scissors are for cutting paper or other art materials. They are never to be used for cutting hair, clothing, or other children.

Easel Brushes
Provide a variety of sizes and styles. Brush handles should not exceed six inches in length. Better brushes are set in seamless aluminum or nickel-plated holders which are rust-proof. They hold bristles well, and their handles are less likely to come loose. Brushes with long bristles have greater flexibility. Provide two types of brushes: rounded and flat ends in sizes ¾ inch to 1¼ inch. Short, stubby brushes with nylon hairs are easy for two- and three-year-olds to use.

Imitating Life: Homeliving and Dramatic Play

reschoolers enjoy pretend play. Pretend play for young preschoolers reflects the roles that are most familiar to them, primarily housekeeping or home-related activities. Activities may include meal preparation, bedtime routines, pretending to be Mommy or Daddy, or even being the family pet. As children's mental abilities grow, their pretend play reflects the capacity to make objects and actions stand for something or someone. Therefore, pretend play centered around a home theme (homeliving) takes on a more dramatic role and is defined as dramatic play. In dramatic play, children use props, plot, and roles to symbolize real or imaginary experiences. Dramatic play focuses on social roles and interactions and reveals children's abilities to play with ideas.

Chapter 9

Values

Physical

- Develops large and small muscles
- Develops eye-hand coordination
- Provides opportunities to use the five senses
- Allows preschoolers time to relax and release energy
- Helps preschoolers become aware of their physical bodies
- Develops skills like pouring and stirring

Mental

- Allows children to engage in problem solving and decision making
- Enriches the child's verbal and nonverbal communication skills
- Helps children construct their own understanding of how the world works
- Lays a foundation for symbolic thinking

Social / Emotional

- Gives children opportunities to cooperate, take turns, and share roles
- Allows children to "try on" roles of people in their lives
- Develops skills in conflict resolution
- Enhances relationships with peers
- Develops the ability to express feelings appropriately
- Allows children to practice negotiation skills
- Helps children feel in control by making things happen
- Promotes feelings of security with the use of familiar materials

Spiritual

- Provides opportunities for children to hear Bible verses and conversation about Bible stories and Bible characters
- Allows children time to process, internalize, and express biblical truths such as: "We can be kind to one another" or "People at church work together."
- Introduces biblical concepts such as, "God planned for families."

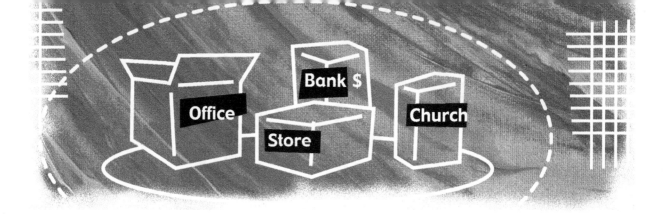

Most children naturally engage in dramatic play between 18 months and 2 years of age. Children begin pretending with trucks, dolls, and dishes. By four or five, their play is more complex and inspired by props and everyday experiences. Fives and sixes are capable of engaging in more complex dramatic play.

Through the course of play, children often express feelings they may not be able to express otherwise—feelings such as fear, insecurity, or even joy. For instance, one Sunday the four-year-olds viewed a car accident from the window in the room. Although no one was seriously injured, police cars and fire trucks arrived. In the homeliving center over the next few weeks, the children played out the accident and pretended to care for the hurt people. By playing out the scene over and over, the preschoolers were learning to cope with their emotions.

Homeliving Center

The homeliving center contributes to the child's feelings of security at church because furnishings and materials are similar to items at home. Guidelines for setting up a homeliving center:
1. Locate the center in a corner of the room clearly visible from the door.
2. Place the center near other noisy centers such as blocks.
3. Consider placing a rug in the center to reduce noise.
4. Attach an unbreakable mirror to the wall.

Many of the same homeliving materials are used in all preschool age groups, but each age group will use the materials differently. For example, infants delight in touching a doll. Older ones carry the doll around the room. Twos rock and hug the doll. Threes dress and undress the doll and pretend to care for the baby. Fours, pre-kindergartners, and kindergartners enjoy turning the homeliving center into a baby nursery at the hospital.

Other homeliving activities include:
• looking in an unbreakable mirror, carrying a purse, wrapping the doll in a blanket, and pretending to talk on a toy phone.
• enjoying simple food preparation experiences, such as spreading soft margarine on bread or toast.
• adding child-sized mops and brooms, doll clothes, wooden cooking spoons, aprons, and dress-up clothes. A toy cash register, play money, discarded telephone, camera, flashlight, and strips of cloth provide opportunities for more complex play.

Preschoolers need space, props, and time to pursue dramatic play. Child-sized furniture and equipment encourages imaginative play. Basic furnishings for the center include a table, stove, sink, wall mirror, two to four chairs, doll bed, and a child-sized rocker.

Guiding Preschoolers in Dramatic Play

Younger preschoolers shift roles and refocus their play frequently because of short attention spans. Engage younger preschoolers in simple conversation as they play in homeliving.

Older preschoolers are more sophisticated in play and become involved in planning and negotiating roles. Older preschoolers may spend almost the entire session in a dramatic play experience. Because of their ability to engage in complex dramatic play, they will transform the center into theme-related play. The center may become a bakery, grocery store, photography studio, or a Bible-related place such as a synagogue, Bible-times home, or marketplace.

Prop Boxes
Store: play money, cash register, bags, tags for prices, shelf labels, purses, wallets
- for grocery store, add empty food containers
- for clothing store, add a variety of dress-up clothes
- for pet store, add various pet food containers and new leashes

Office: telephone, adding machine, computer keyboard, paper, hole punch
- for business office, add briefcase and file folders
- for church office, add Bible, bulletins, and offering envelopes
- for library, add books, index cards, stamp, and washable stamp pad

Need a new doll? Look for a plastic baby doll with molded hair and few moving parts.

Guidelines for Teachers

1. Use pictures, stories, or visitors to give children the information they need to pretend. Children need to be familiar with roles before enacting them. For example, before children engage in play for setting up a Bible-times market, provide pictures of what a market might have looked like along, with pictures or samples of the kinds of foods available.
2. Make the center's physical setting appealing and inviting. Neatly arrange dress-up items and other props. Keep clothes and props clean and sanitized. Provide hooks, shelves, or other storage for props.
3. Provide adequate props for play. Dress-up clothes should be easy to put on and not too long. (Hint: Children's clothing two or three sizes larger is just right.) Guide preschoolers to always wear socks with dress-up shoes. Avoid any jewelry.
4. Guide play with conversation, but intervene only when necessary.

Homeliving and the Child with Special Needs

- Encourage preschoolers to include the child with special needs. Help preschoolers know when to help the child and when to allow him to do the activity on his own.
- Model how to communicate with the child.
- Verbally state the child's desire in acceptable ways.
- Encourage the child to try activities that require new skills.

Cooking with Preschoolers

Cooking is a favorite activity for preschoolers. Cooking experiences can be incorporated into a homeliving/dramatic play center in a variety of ways. Younger preschoolers enjoy following simple recipes. Cooking can incorporate theme-related play, such as a bakery center or restaurant center. Use these guidelines as you cook with preschoolers:

1. Supervise cooking activities at all times.
2. Place an electric skillet in a box that has edges the same height as the edges of the skillet. Place a rolled terry cloth towel in the spaces between the skillet and the box.
3. Locate electrical appliances next to an outlet to avoid tripping over a cord.
4. Use short-handled wooden or plastic spoons for stirring.
5. Place a plastic tablecloth underneath the table for easier cleanup.
6. Inform parents of cooking or tasting activities by placing a sign outside the room door. Ask parents about allergies to the food items being used. (Many preschoolers are especially allergic to peanut butter, chocolate, and milk products.)
7. Let children measure, pour, stir, and taste.
8. Teachers and children should always wash their hands before beginning to cook.
9. Have pot holders and oven mitts available.
10. Turn off appliances such as toaster ovens and electric skillets when not in use.
11. Avoid cooking with honey for younger preschoolers.

The following foods can cause choking in preschoolers and should not be used in preschool departments

Nuts	Popcorn
Carrots (unless finely shredded)	Peanut butter (unless in a recipe)
Grapes (unless cut into quarters)	Hot dogs
Celery	Unpeeled fruits such as apples and pears
Marshmallows	Peanuts

No-Cook Recipes

Butter
Allow whipping cream to come to room temperature. Put two tablespoons of cream in a small plastic jar and shake until butter is formed. Strain the liquid. Serve on salted crackers or add a small amount of salt to the butter.

Fruit Pops (3's—Pre-K)
1 cup bananas (2 medium, sliced)
10 oz. frozen berries (strawberries, blueberries, whatever you like)
1½ cups crushed pineapple with juice
⅔ cup evaporated milk
Put ingredients in a blender and mix well. Pour into five-ounce paper cups. Place a craft stick in each cup and freeze.

Simple Snacks
- Spread saltine crackers with cream cheese and vanilla frosting.
- Use a pretzel stick to dip sliced bananas into dry gelatin.

Shakes
- Fill a baby food jar half full of milk. Add one teaspoon of instant pudding. Shake until the mixture is thick. Eat!
- Fill a baby food jar half full of applesauce. Add one teaspoon of dry gelatin and shake until the gelatin dissolves.
- Put two tablespoons of ice cream in a baby food jar. Fill remainder of jar with milk. Shake to make a milkshake.
- Fill a baby food jar half full of diced bananas. Add one teaspoon of dry gelatin and shake until bananas are coated.

The Bible has much to say about our relationships with family members, friends, and others in the community. The homeliving/dramatic play center provides an abundance of opportunities for us to share these biblical truths with preschoolers and help them realize how these truths apply to their daily lives. In the homeliving/dramatic play center, a child may begin to discover, "I can do what the Bible says!"—and that is a wondrous discovery indeed.

Building Blocks: Blocks and Construction

Morgan bounced into the preschool room with her two best friends, William and Joseph. They moved quickly from Bible-learning center to Bible-learning center. Finally, they arrived in the block center. I had placed several animal and people figures, along with some small branches placed in clay, to support the session's Bible story about Adam and Eve taking care of the animals. Morgan had other ideas. She said to me: "Hey, we are going to do a show. Do you want to help?" I normally refuse to do any more than assist, but I was caught up in the moment. I nodded my head. She gave me the job of raising the pretend curtain. She announced that she would be Mrs. Noah and William would be Mr. Noah. She said that Joseph would be the Laughters. I asked her who the Laughters were. She said, "You know, those people who laughed at Noah for doing what God wanted him to do." She told me to raise the curtain. I raised the curtain with the sound, "Dadada!" She frowned and said: "No sounds, please. Just raise the curtain." I did as I was told. When the curtain raised, Morgan, William, and Joseph began to make rain sounds and waves with their arms. Then, Morgan said: "We forgot the boat. Let's build the boat." They worked to build an enclosure, making sure that all the animals and appropriate people were in the boat. The saga continued. As the rain fell again, Joseph slapped his people figures that were not on the boat down on the floor. I did not even ask. Then the rain motion stopped. Joseph stood and arched his hands above his head in a large motion. I asked, "Tell me about what you are doing?" He responded: "It's the rainbow. God said He would not send the flood again." I replied: "Noah obeyed God and took care of the animals. Adam and Eve took care of the animals. William, Joseph, and Morgan can obey God by helping at home."

Even though Morgan, William, and Joseph did not play out the Bible story for the session, it was still a worthwhile Bible-learning experience that eventually led to the biblical truth that we can obey God. This story demonstrates why blocks are such an important avenue for teaching about God.

> "Next to water, sand, and mud, the most valuable play material for young children is likely to be blocks."[1]

Water

Sand

Mud

Blocks

Physical

- Strengthens and develops control of large and small muscles as preschoolers reach, stretch, and change positions while building
- Develops eye-hand coordination
- Provides tools for a child to create visuals that include symmetry, balance, and patterns

Mental

- Encourages creativity as a child chooses what to build
- Develops problem-solving skills as a child discovers how to build
- Helps teach pre-math skills such as ordering, counting, sorting, fractions, and measurements
- Begins basic understanding of science including gravity, force, and matter
- Develops reasoning skills through cause and effect

Social / Emotional

- Provides opportunities to communicate, resolve conflicts, and respect others
- Provides preschoolers opportunities to work together as they build or put away the blocks
- Allows preschoolers to role-play life events
- Builds relationships with teachers and other children
- Encourages initiative and ownership

Spiritual

- Allows preschoolers to role-play Bible stories
- Provides preschoolers opportunities to hear Bible story conversation, Bible verses and phrases, and songs
- Offers opportunities for teachers to observe biblical understanding and to answer Bible-related questions

Developing Block Building Skills

Having a general understanding of the stages of block building will help teachers understand what to expect from preschoolers, how to plan, and how to assist the child. The following statements are generally true, but remember, preschoolers move through the same stages but at different rates. (See pages 76-77 for a description of the types of blocks to use for each age group.)

Babies

- may use small blocks (larger than the child's fist) for dump-and-fill.
- may taste, touch, and smell blocks.

One-year-olds

- carry blocks, learning how to hold onto them, how heavy they feel, and how they sound when they fall.
- create piles of blocks in different areas of the room.

Two-year-olds

- begin construction that is impulsive and with no preset plan.
- make a simple tower by stacking blocks unevenly, then knocking them down with delight.
- lay blocks side-by-side on the floor.
- build horizontally by placing blocks end-to-end.
- repeat patterns over and over.
- show through their block play that building is a process, not a product or thing.
- play with blocks alone.

Three-year-olds

- continue to enjoy building as a process that often involves using every block in the block center.
- create first bridges by standing or laying two blocks on their sides, placing a third block across the top.
- build based on previous experience or knowledge with bridging. The bridge is completed to create an enclosure that resembles rooms, pens, or yards.
- repeat forms throughout their block structures.
- discover elements of balancing.
- play alone or near other children, but rarely in cooperation with one another.

Four-year-olds

- decorate structures with patterns, symmetry, and rhythm.
- combine enclosures and bridges to make more complex structures.
- make a series of bridges.
- begin to name the structure, but their structure may not resemble the actual place. The child may not start with a plan or name in mind. Naming often occurs at the end of the building process.
- use blocks as settings for dramatic play involving figures of people, animals, and cars.
- begin creating very simple structures or things that stand for something else. Symbols are very concrete.
- start working together, but cooperation may be difficult at times.

Five- and six-year-olds

- plan systematically by deciding what they want to build and by naming the structure before they begin.
- build elaborate structures that imitate the real world.
- build cooperatively with other preschoolers.
- create a structure individually, but then link with other structures in cooperative play.
- print labels for buildings or create stories around the building.

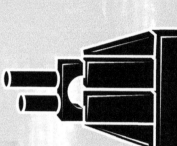

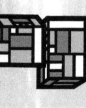

Discussing Block Structures

Things teachers should not say:
- "What are you building?"
- "That looks great!"
- "That looks like a church."
- "Let me show you what to build."

Before discussing structures, observe these things:
- What blocks were used?
- Where were the blocks placed?
- How were the blocks balanced?
- How were the blocks used?
- What props were used in building?
- Which blocks were used the same way?
- Which blocks were used in different ways?
- How were blocks connected?
- Was the child looking at a Bible-teaching picture?

Comment on structures in the following ways:
- "You used the longest blocks in the block center."
- "Tell me how you placed the blocks so that they would balance."
- "That structure reminds me of our Bible story. Mary and Joseph did not have a house to sleep in for the night. They had to sleep in a stable."

Setting up the Block Center

- Provide a low shelf with vertical subdivisions.
- Place in low-traffic area.
- Make the center visible from other parts of the room.
- Locate away from doorways.
- Provide space large enough for four or five children to play.
- Place on low pile carpet or hardwood floor.
- Use the walls or the shelf as a way to define the area.
- For wooden blocks, develop a storage arrangement system with matching puzzle bases. Trace the block shapes and accessories on poster board and mount the board to areas of the block shelf with clear contact paper. Thus, blocks can be sorted by size. When blocks are being put away, cleanup becomes a giant puzzle.
- Place the largest blocks on the lower shelves.
- Create a vehicle parking area.
- Display small pieces in clear plastic containers.
- Define the area for building. An area rug or vinyl tablecloth will help define the area. Masking tape can be used.

Placing two double-unit wooden blocks at right angles in an obvious spot will usually draw attention to the block center. Even preschoolers hate unfinished work.[2]

When children begin playing with wooden blocks, consider providing a "no play" zone in front of the shelf to keep children from knocking down structures when reaching for additional blocks.

75

Equipment for the Block Center

Blockbusters®—A brand name for cardboard blocks that are durable and easy to handle. These blocks are best for babies through two-year-olds.

Unit Blocks—Unit blocks were first developed in 1914 by Carolyn Pratt in New York City. These wooden blocks come in a variety of shapes—rectangles, squares, triangles, cylinders, half circles, quarter circles, arches, and a lot more. The single-unit block is the starting block. It is 1⅜ inches by 2½ inches by 5½ inches. All other blocks relate to the size of the single-unit block—two single-unit blocks make a double-unit block, two double-unit blocks make one quadruple-unit block, and so on. These blocks are great for beginning building; they help preschoolers master distance, balance, and measurement easier than random-sized blocks. Unit blocks make it easy for a child to build a bridge or an enclosure because the blocks match mathematically. The unit and its subsequent units help a child with good beginning math skills. In the block center, preschoolers begin working with fractions.

Duplos®, *Legos*®, *and other specialty building blocks/materials*—Other types of building resources may be best used separately from unit blocks. Legos® and unit blocks sometimes do not work well together. Place these materials in another area of the room on a plastic tablecloth for easy cleanup.

> Preschoolers speak with blocks. They say what they have to say. The question is, "Are we listening?"

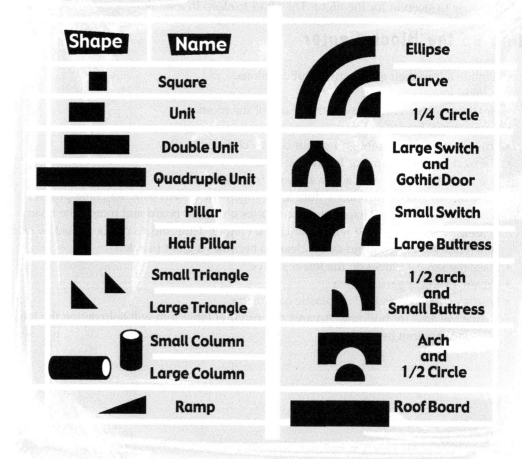

Use these guidelines for the number of blocks to use for your age group:

Babies – A few small blocks (larger than the child's fist) or a few Blockbusters

Ones and twos – 12 Blockbusters or shoe box size cardboard blocks

Threes – 60 to 70 wooden unit blocks in 7 to 12 shapes

Fours—Kindergarten – 150 wooden unit blocks in 19 to 27 shapes

Make your own blocks

Milk Carton Blocks—Use clean plastic or cardboard milk cartons. Fill with paper and tape closed.

Baby Wipes Blocks—Use plastic baby wipe containers. Fill with paper and tape closed.

Shoe Box Blocks—Fill shoe boxes with newspaper and tape closed.

Paper Sack Blocks—Preschoolers can decorate the bags, then fill with newspaper, fold top, and tape closed.

Accessories for Block Play

Carpet squares	Cardboard cylinders
Fabric pieces	Hard hats
Traffic signs	Short pieces of yarn
Modeling clay	Film canisters
Flashlights	Empty thread spools
Batting for snow or clouds	Blankets
Coffee cans and lids	Cardboard boxes of various sizes
Poster board, construction paper	Seashells
Plastic tubing	Stones
PVC piping and fittings	

Vehicles—large and small boats, cars, trucks, buses, and airplanes

Plastic strawberry baskets with the bottoms cut out for animals fences

Animal and people (multiethnic) figures

Paper grass (used in Easter baskets)

Guiding and Teaching Through Block Play

- Provide block play throughout the Bible-learning time.
- Limit the number of children to four or five or whatever your space will allow.
- Use Bible story conversation, Bible stories, and Bible verses to reinforce Bible truths.
- Guide preschoolers to take blocks down one at a time or to request permission to knock down only their own structures.
- Straighten up the block center occasionally when there is a break in play.
- Allow preschoolers to leave up their structure for group time.
- Direct preschoolers not to walk on blocks (except for a balance beam).
- Do not allow preschoolers to kick down blocks, throw blocks, or use blocks for guns.
- Help children understand that accidents happen sometimes.

Block-building Basics

Some simple guidelines for preschoolers can help make block play less stressful:
- Build no higher than your chin.
- Build only in the block center.
- Build on the floor.
- Build with blocks rather than throwing, pushing, or kicking them.
- Build far enough from the shelf to allow others to use the blocks.
- Build with only your blocks. Never take from a friend's structure without asking.

Using Blocks with Preschoolers with Special Needs

Blocks can be used with all preschoolers. Use these ideas to adapt block play:

For preschoolers who have difficulty seeing:
- Introduce blocks slowly, gradually increasing the number of blocks, giving them a small variety of shapes and sizes at first.
- Trace and cut out block shapes on textured poster board or sandpaper. Mount the shaped poster board in the block shelf. This will aid in cleanup. A child can feel the location of the blocks. It will help him know where to find the blocks to build during the session.
- Use simple words and phrases that are descriptive: "This is a square block."

For preschoolers who have difficulty hearing:
- Help with language. Sign the rules and help the child understand what is expected in block play. Assist in negotiating with other children.
- Encourage other children to look directly at the child when speaking.

For preschoolers who have difficulty sitting in the block center:
- Allow the child to rest on the floor with a bolster pillow under his chest.
- Place the child near the block shelf or bring blocks to the child.
- Allow the child to sit in a corner where two walls can support a sitting position for a time.
- Allow the child to have a building tray on his wheelchair.
- Encourage horizontal building.

For preschoolers with limited comprehension:
- Introduce blocks gradually. Give five blocks of the same size and same shape. Increase the number gradually.
- Offer lots of encouragement.
- Allow enough time for cleanup and transition. Change may not be easy for this child.

[1] Baxter, Katherine Read, and Fane, Xenia F. *Understanding and Guiding Young Children* (Englewood Cliffs: Prentice-Hall, Inc., 1967), 189.
[2] Hirsch, Elisabeth, ed. *The Block Book* (Washington, D.C.: National Association for the Education of Young Children, 1984), 93-94.

Putting the Pieces Together: Puzzles and Manipulatives

aroline loved puzzles. It did not matter what other activities were offered; the first thing Caroline did was work every puzzle in the room. She could master a new puzzle in a matter of minutes. She not only loved wooden and floor puzzles, but as she grew older, she also loved word and math puzzles. Puzzles are the most common type of manipulative used with preschoolers. Manipulatives are toys and materials that aid in the fine motor development of the hands, wrists, and fingers. Manipulatives include materials such as puzzles, games, beads, pegboards, and small blocks such as Duplos®, Legos®, and Lincoln Logs®.

Puzzles and manipulatives stimulate the mental, physical, social, emotional, and spiritual growth of preschoolers. Manipulatives offer preschoolers opportunities to string beads, make patterns, match, sort, classify, stack, sequence, count, and work with colors and shapes. As preschoolers master manipulative skills, they gain confidence to try new activities and seek greater challenges.

Values

Physical

- Develop fine motor skills and eye-hand coordination
- Help develop handwriting dexterity

Mental

- Stimulate conversation and increase vocabulary
- Develop thinking, matching, and recognition skills
- Allow left-to-right sequencing when puzzle pieces are placed on the left side of the puzzle
- Challenge preschoolers when puzzles vary in difficulty
- Develop problem-solving skills as preschoolers discover one or more ways to use the materials
- Provide opportunities to associate, match, classify, and sequence

Social / Emotional

- Encourage social interaction and cooperation
- Provide opportunities for teacher and child to talk
- Promote self-confidence and satisfaction by working with different materials
- Provide opportunities for preschoolers to work alone
- Provide opportunities to learn responsibility for returning materials to the shelf
- Enhance feelings of satisfaction, self-confidence, and competence

Spiritual

- Provide opportunities to hear Bible story conversation, verses, stories, and songs
- Provide opportunities for preschoolers to work together, requiring cooperation and sharing
- Allow preschoolers to make choices
- Develop Bible reading readiness

Types of Puzzles and Manipulatives

Preschoolers as young as nine months enjoy simple pull-apart, put-together, and reactive manipulatives. Snap-lock beads, linking toys, and stacking rings are examples of pull-apart and put-together manipulatives for babies. Reactive manipulatives allow babies to perform a task (such as pushing a button) and receive a reaction. Activity centers, pop-up toys, and music boxes are examples of reactive manipulatives. Babies also find simple puzzles, such as a fill-and-dump bottle, fascinating and enjoyable. As babies and ones grow, they can master nesting cups and shape sorter toys. Placing the receiver on a toy phone is a simple toddler puzzle. Manipulatives for two-year-olds consist of matching pictures, folding doll clothes, and stacking mixing bowls. Threes, fours, and pre-kindergartners enjoy working floor puzzles, sorting nuts or buttons, and playing simple concentration games. Kindergartners continue to develop skills with puzzles that allow them to use pattern cards to string beads, sequence Bible story pictures, and make their own Bible verse puzzles.

Puzzles
The wooden in-lay puzzle is the most common type of puzzle used with preschoolers. Threes through kindergartners find large floor puzzles challenging. Whole piece puzzles are most appropriate for ones and young twos. Offer puzzles that are suitable for your age group.

Age	Number of Pieces
Ones—Twos	2-6 pieces
Older Twos—Threes	2-11 pieces
Older Threes, Fours, Pre-Ks	10-24 pieces
Kindergartners	11-30 pieces

Many challenging and appropriate puzzles can be made from household items.

Cereal Box Puzzle—Cut the front panels from preschoolers' favorite cereal boxes. Cover with clear contact plastic or laminate and cut each panel into several pieces. The number of pieces depends on the age of the preschoolers in your class/department. As a variation, place magnetic tape on the puzzle pieces and guide preschoolers to work the puzzle on a metal (not aluminum) cookie sheet.

Photo Puzzle—Enlarge one or two photographs of the children involved in Bible-learning activities. Glue the photographs to poster board. Cut them into the number of pieces appropriate for your age group. Pre-kindergartners and kindergartners find homemade floor puzzles challenging.

Reactive Manipulatives— a toy which elicits a physical response or reaction from the child to do something

Construction, Pull-apart and Put-together Toys

Nesting cups, pegs and pegboards, and assorted sizes and colors of beads or buttons for lacing and sorting provide opportunities for the child to interact and engage in Bible story as teachers use Bible story conversation.

Working with manipulatives such as interlocking blocks and construction toys allows older preschoolers to be creative. Manipulatives such as these are open-ended. Unlike puzzles that have only one way of fitting together, these manipulatives can be used in a variety of ways. Duplos®, Legos®, Lincoln Logs®, Tinkertoys®, geoboards, bristle blocks, magnetic blocks, and parquetry blocks are examples of construction-type manipulatives.

Nuts and Bolts—Gather a variety of nuts and bolts. Separate the nuts and bolts and place them in individual containers. Older preschoolers can assemble, sort, or weigh the items. Add a ruler to the center for children to measure the length of the bolts.

Cotton Ball Pickup—Purchase a bag of multicolor cotton balls, an ice cube tray, a shallow bowl, and tongs. Place cotton balls in bowl. Demonstrate to the child how to pick up a cotton ball with the bread tongs and place it in an ice tray compartment.

Geoboard—Purchase a piece of pegboard, nuts and bolts to fit the holes in the pegboard, and different sizes and colors of rubber bands. Cut the pegboard into 12-by-12-inch squares. Push the bolts through all the holes and secure them with the nuts. The top of the geoboard is the side with the bolt ends protruding. Guide the children to make designs by overlapping the rubber bands on the bolts. To ensure safety, purchase bolts with flat heads and ends.

Magnetic Board—Purchase an adhesive-backed 12-by-12-inch magnetic sheet at your local craft or discount store. Peel the back from the sheet and press it onto the lid of a boot-sized shoe box. Place magnetic letters, numbers, or shapes inside the box.

Games

A variety of games require manipulative skills. Games for preschoolers should be played in a cooperative, rather than competitive, manner with simple and flexible rules. Picture and texture dominoes as well as memory and concentration games encourage matching, sorting, and classifying.

Shape Sorting Game—From colorful construction paper, cut several different sizes and colors of squares, triangles, and circles. Gather three sheets of white card stock and glue one of the shapes to the top of each page. Place the remaining shapes in a pie tin. Invite the children to choose a shape out of the pie tin and match it to a shape card. *Variation for older preschoolers:* Add shapes such as ovals, diamonds, rectangles, or even trapezoids. Make a shape chart on poster board. Divide the poster into squares with one square for each shape; print the name of a shape in each square. Place the shapes in a paper bag and allow the children to draw a shape and match it to the shape chart.

Sorting Games—Gather large buttons, beads, keys, or assorted nuts. Give older preschoolers colorful plastic bowls or an egg carton for sorting.

Listening Game—Locate four film canisters. Add rice to one, small rocks to another, salt or sand to the third, and dried beans to the fourth. Make a gameboard by gluing or taping some of each item onto a piece of construction paper. Guide children to shake each container gently, determine which item it contains, and place it on the gameboard.

Card and Envelope Match—Collect various sizes and shapes of greeting cards with matching envelopes. Place the cards in one basket and the envelopes in another basket. The children can match each card to its envelope. Be sure the illustrations on the cards are realistic and appropriate for preschoolers. Choose the number of cards appropriate for your age group.

Number/Counting Block—Create a number block to use with games by stuffing a small square box with newspaper, securing the sides and tops with tape, and covering the box with solid color of contact plastic. Place a number of dots on each side of the box to represent the numberals 1 through 6.

Setting Up the Manipulatives/Puzzles Center

The location and setup of the center may determine whether or not preschoolers choose puzzles and manipulatives during the session. Consider the following guidelines for setting up the center:

- Place puzzles in a quiet area of the room, out of the main traffic area.
- Offer two or three puzzles per session. Enhance the puzzles and manipulatives center by placing each puzzle on a sheet of construction paper, a place mat, or a carpet square.
- Store manipulatives such as beads and put-together blocks in their own dishpan or plastic container. For kindergartners, place a picture or word label on the container showing the toy and its name.
- Provide more than one set of the most popular manipulatives.
- Use puzzles and manipulatives in other learning centers when appropriate.
- Check to be sure wooden puzzles are free of splinters, sharp edges, toxic paint, and small pieces that could be swallowed.
- Print a word or number on the back of each puzzle piece that matches a word or number on the back of the corresponding puzzle board. Stray or mixed-up pieces can be easily returned to the correct board.
- Use puzzles that depict realistic objects, animals, and people instead of fantasy figures. Realistic pictures help reinforce Bible truths.
- Store puzzles in large ziplock bags to keep the pieces together.

One of the best ways to ensure that a preschooler has positive experiences with puzzles and manipulatives is for you to sit beside the child as he works. Preschoolers enjoy conversation and interaction with adults. The time you spend with a child helps you understand and know the child better.

Guidelines for Puzzle and Manipulative Experiences

- Guide preschoolers to remove puzzle pieces one at a time and place them to the left of the frame. Working puzzles from left to right helps develop reading readiness.
- Allow preschoolers to work at their own speed. Make puzzles and manipulatives available for children of differing abilities.
- Use the Bible in the learning center and use Bible story conversation, Bible phrases and verses, and songs.
- Remind preschoolers to complete the puzzle or put manipulatives back in their containers before moving to another activity.
- Help or encourage another preschooler to give assistance if a child becomes frustrated with a puzzle.
- Add excitement to the puzzle center by encouraging preschoolers to put puzzles together in different ways, such as putting a wooden puzzle together outside the frame.
- Change the puzzles and manipulatives often.
- Look for simple concentration, sequencing, patterning, and construction items to enhance the area.
- Find ways to incorporate puzzles and manipulatives in other areas of the room, such as patterning blocks in the nature center.
- Introduce a new puzzle by talking about the picture on the puzzle and the color and shape of the puzzle pieces.
- Help children work puzzles with questions such as, "What is missing?" and "Where does the largest piece go?"

Manipulatives and puzzles are effective tools for teaching biblical truths. Recent research indicates that the brain naturally seeks to make sense of our experiences and connect them to other known information. By providing a variety of materials that meet different skill levels, teachers are able to relate each child's experiences to Bible phrases, Bible story conversation, Bible stories, and Bible characters. This learning environment enables preschoolers to not only encounter Bible truths, but to internalize them and apply them to daily life as well.

Exploring God's Creation: Nature and Science

Chapter 12

s Joshua looked up in the sky and saw a double rainbow, he shouted, "Look Mommy, God painted two rainbows in the sky." Joshua had an "aha" moment. God's creation is full of wonder and joy. What could be a more natural way to teach preschoolers about God? Through nature and science, preschoolers can begin to understand that God created the world for them to enjoy and can learn to care for God's world.

Values

Physical

- Develop large and small motor skills
- Allow preschoolers to use their senses
- Help teach responsibility as children care for plants and animals
- Develop eye-hand coordination

Mental

- Increase vocabulary
- Enhance awareness of the world God made
- Help preschoolers learn about the natural world
- Allow preschoolers to explore, question, experiment, discover truths, and form ideas

Social / Emotional

- Provide opportunities for social interaction and cooperation
- Stimulate conversation
- Encourage preschoolers to enjoy and appreciate God's world
- Provide moments of awe and wonder

Spiritual

- Provide a natural venue for teachers to use Bible verses, Bible stories, songs, and books
- Provide opportunities for learning about God by experiencing His creation
- Teach respect for living things
- Encourage preschoolers to worship as they experience the wonder of God's world

Nature and science centers are viewed where little activity takes place. In fact, teachers may not give much attention to the center. However, you can utilize nature items to stimulate the senses and create natural learning experiences about God. From birth, preschoolers explore their environment. As children respond to their surroundings, teachers can begin teaching them about God's world through Bible story conversation and simple songs. As the preschoolers grow older, teachers can use nature and science activities to build on preschoolers' natural curiosity and to stimulate imagination and creativity. Young children become excited about nature and science when they are given the opportunity to explore and interact with God's creation. As a teacher, your goal is to help preschoolers become active investigators of God's world. You can nurture a child's observation skills, classification skills, and estimation and prediction skills through appropriate nature and science activities.

Guiding Nature/Science Experiences

- Allow preschoolers time to interact with the nature materials. Children need to explore, experiment, examine, and experience the wonder of God's creation.
- Provide activities and experiences that do not require much teacher guidance; children should be able to do the activities themselves.
- Provide a balance of individual and group activities.
- Permit the children to get their hands dirty.
- Go outside whenever possible to experience God's world. When circumstances prevent walking outside, bring nature items inside.
- Encourage responsibility by letting older preschoolers care for plants and small animals (fish).
- Allow children to discover a nature item before showing it to them. Discovery encourages the physical, logical, and natural learners to grow.
- Give simple answers to preschoolers' questions about nature. The child will ask for more information when he needs it. If you give too much information initially, you may discourage children's questions and curiosity.
- Avoid using the word *magic* when referring to natural processes. Explain that God planned for seed to grow or for water to freeze and make ice.

Providing Safe Nature Experiences

When using nature and science with preschoolers, remember that hygiene and safety are important. Always wash hands after handling nature items such as animals, birds' nests, and plants. Since younger preschoolers tend to put their hands in their mouths, keep a small dishpan of soapy water or moist baby wipes near nature materials so hands can be cleaned. Be aware of preschoolers' allergies. Some children may have reactions to small animals, certain foods,

Science in the early years is an extension of sensory experiences (seeing, hearing, tasting, touching, smelling).

Preschoolers already have the most important tools for investigating nature—their senses.

and floral scents. You may want to ask parents to complete a health form that includes information about known food, animal, and scent allergies. Parents can describe the allergic reaction, such as, "Marcy will have difficulty breathing." Some allergies may not be known, since a child may not have had contact with the allergen. Watch for any reactions to the items you provide in the nature and science center. Mild allergic reactions include sneezing, watery eyes, and itching. A severe reaction may also cause difficulty in breathing. Whenever you are using unusual items in the nature and science center (or other centers), use an allergy alert notice to notify parents. The notice could read like this:

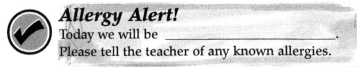

Allergy Alert!
Today we will be _____.
Please tell the teacher of any known allergies.

Sometimes allergic reactions can appear from unexpected sources. Matthew was highly allergic to peanuts and any products that contained peanuts. If a peanut touched the tabletop and Matthew then touched the table, he would have a severe reaction. Matthew's teacher brought prepackaged sunflower seeds for the children to taste and explore in the nature center. After setting up the activity, the teacher looked at the ingredients listed on the package of sunflower seed. She was shocked to find the words "May contain peanut oil." Matthew could have had an allergic reaction from an unlikely source.

Safety Tips

- Read ingredients of prepackaged foods before using with preschoolers.
- Do not allow preschoolers to touch reptiles. They may carry salmonella.
- Place a bird's nest in a clear, closed container.
- Smooth sharp edges of shells with sandpaper.
- Closely supervise small nature items since they could pose a choking hazard.
- Place leaves and flowers in a clear container or plastic bag for younger preschoolers.

Poisonous Plants

Azalea	Jerusalem Cherry
Bird of Paradise	Lantana
Burning Bush	Larkspur
Caladium	Lily of the Valley
Caster Bean	Mistletoe
Columbine	Mock Orange
Cyclamen	Morning Glory
Daffodil	Mountain Laurel
Delphinium	Narcissus
Dieffenbachia	Oleander
Elephant Ears	Philodendron
English Ivy	Pinks
Four O' Clock	Poinsettia
Hens and Chickens	Potato
Holly	Rhododendron
Hyacinth	Scotch Broom
Iris	Spider Lily
Ivy	Sweet Pea

Check with your agricultural extension for poisonous plants in your area.

Setting up a Nature/Science Center

Choose an area close to a window for the nature and science center. If a window is not available, place the center in a quiet area in the room. You may want to place the center near a sink, if available, so a water source is readily available. Display nature items on a window sill or short shelf. For kindergartners, consider adding a table. Often, a table encourages group projects.

Keep your eyes open for collectible nature items. Ask parents or grandparents who travel to be on the lookout for unusual items. For example, if you live in an area without colorful fall leaves, encourage people who visit other areas to bring fall leaves for teachers to share. Other items to collect for the nature center are:

small rocks	shells	hay
dried flowers	seed packets	clear containers
textured fabric	sand	magnifying glass
cork	nature pictures	magnets
rulers	scales	watering can

Your nature and science center can be a fun center for exploring God's world and learning Bible truths. But you must keep the center interesting. Change nature items regularly. Set up a nature and science display, a group of related items, to stimulate curiosity. For example, you could create a display of pinecones. Include pinecones of various sizes and types. Add pictures of pine trees. You could even add a pine branch with pinecones still attached. Place a Bible opened to an appropriate verse. Think of other ways to create interest in the center. Display items on pieces of construction paper; arrange items in baskets; place a tool caddy in the center for rulers, magnifying glasses, and other items; add pencils or crayons and paper so children can note their observations; provide nature books and magazines to enhance exploration and learning.

Enjoying Nature Outdoors

Take the opportunity, as circumstances permit, to help preschoolers enjoy nature experiences outdoors. A small garden in the corner of your playground can help you teach. Older preschoolers can learn the benefits and consequences of caring or not caring for God's world. Caring for a small garden teaches preschoolers the cycle of life as they plant flower seed, watch flowers emerge from the ground, see flowers drop seed, observe flowers die, and see flowers emerge again the next year. In your garden, use plants native to your area. Include bird feeders for more learning opportunities.

Nature walks provide other outdoor learning experiences. Babies and ones can enjoy the outside world when their teachers take them on short walks or for a ride in a stroller. Twos and threes enjoy collecting nature items in paper bags or on "nature bracelets" (masking tape around the wrist, sticky side out). Fours, pre-kindergartners, and kindergartners may enjoy nature scavenger hunts when teachers provide a list of items to find.

Guidelines for Nature Walks

- Always have at least two adults on the walk.
- If walking outside a fenced area, children should hold hands or a rope.
- Before going outside, stress that preschoolers must stay with the group.
- Leave a note on your door to let parents know where you are and when you will return.
- Be aware of any allergies.
- Children should only pick up items from the ground, not pull from trees or bushes.
- Children should wash their hands when they return from the walk.

Ideas for Nature Walks

Match the Color—Give each child a small square of colored paper. Tell the children to look for nature objects that are the same color as their paper squares.

Match the Pictures—Create a "nature walk card" by drawing or gluing pictures of several nature objects found outside. Include items such as a bird, grass, worm, bug, sun, tree, flower, water, or squirrel. Photocopy and laminate the cards. Give each child a card and a crayon. Guide children to mark off each item as they see it.

Catch a Spider Web—Gather dark poster board, white spray paint, and a pair of scissors. Locate a vacant spider web within easy reach and away from anything you don't want to paint. Check the direction of the breeze. Spray the web thoroughly with paint. Position the paper on the other side of the web and gently bring it toward you until the wet web adheres to the paper. Hold the paper steady against the web and snip the foundation strands around the paper to release the web. Allow the web to dry. Spray with clear acrylic to preserve the web. Small webs can be put in clear acetate sheets, and larger webs can be stored in flat gift boxes.

Make a Nature Book—Guide children to collect a variety of nature items on a walk. The children can glue the nature items onto stiff paper. Place the nature items inside ziplock bags. Punch holes in the bags on the ziplock side. Thread a piece of yarn through the holes and tie several bags together to make a book.

Use Homemade Bubble Wands—Create a variety of bubbles by using potato mashers, berry baskets, plastic hair curlers, spools, twisted chenille stems, or small colanders with bubble solution.

If circumstances prevent nature walks, provide similar experiences in the room. For example, you could go on an indoor scavenger hunt. Collect different kinds of leaves and greenery (enough so that each child can make a nature collage after the hunt). Hide the leaves and greenery around the room. On a set of index cards, glue or tape a sample of each nature item. Invite each preschooler to choose a card. The children can search for items that match their cards. When preschoolers find all the different kinds of greenery, give them a piece of poster board to make a collage.

Guiding Science Experiences

All preschoolers are curious about their world. A baby drops a cracker to discover what happens when it hits the floor. A one-year-old removes and replaces the lid to a shoe box. Younger preschoolers have questions and explore to find solutions. When preschoolers start to talk, they begin to *ask* questions. Two- and three-year-olds want to know *what* things are. As they become older, their curiosity turns to wanting to know *why* things happen. For kindergartners, the why questions turn to *how*.

Teachers can join preschoolers on this journey of discovery and encourage their questions. Simple science experiments provide opportunities for preschoolers to fulfill their natural eagerness to find solutions to their questions. Using science experiments can help older preschoolers begin to understand cause and effect, part of the answer to "Why?"

Guidelines for Using Science Experiences with Preschoolers
- Use activities that will allow the children to succeed.
- Try activities before using them with children.
- Encourage children to observe and ask questions.
- Place all materials and tools for the activity in the center.
- Allow children plenty of time to observe, explore, and discover.
- Use books and pictures to give information about science and nature activities.
- Ask open-ended questions to encourage preschoolers to think.
- Include resources (pencils, crayons, paper) for children to record their observations.

Science activities involve a process of observing, classifying, discovering, and communicating. Children can predict what will happen and then test their ideas. They can organize objects or information, classifying similar objects or observations. They can communicate what they discover through drawings, charts, graphs, or words. Tools for science experiences include measuring spoons, measuring cups, scales, magnifying glasses, flashlights, clear containers, large and small mirrors, prisms, eyedroppers, thermometers, rulers, tubs, magnets, and spoons. Look around the house for other items that can be used in simple science activities, such as levers, pulleys, a kitchen scale, or a tuning fork.

All children learn by interacting with their world. Through nature/science activities, you can help a child make the connection between his world and the God who created it.

Science experiments and activities can be divided into these categories:
* Magnets
* Water
* Sand
* Rocks/Soil
* Wind
* Light
* Colors
* Food/Taste
* Measurement

Easy Science Activities

Magnet Painting—Place a sheet of paper in a paper plate. Drop several drops of different colors of tempera paint. Place a small round magnet in the plate. Give the child another magnet. Hold plate up off the table and encourage the child to move the magnet under the plate. Watch as the magnet in the plate moves the paint around.

Weighing Objects—Gather several small objects from around the room. Prepare a chart with a picture or drawing of each object. Using a kitchen scale to weigh each object to see which one weighs the less and which one weighs more. List your results on a chart.

Listening, Singing, and Moving: Music and Movement

 raise the Lord.
Praise God in his holy temple. Praise him in his mighty heavens.
Praise him for his powerful acts.
Praise him because he is greater than anything else.
Praise him by blowing trumpets. Praise him with harps and lyres.
Praise him with tambourine and dancing.
Praise him with stringed instruments and flutes.
Praise him with clashing cymbals. Praise him with clanging cymbals.
Let everything that has breath praise the Lord.
Praise the Lord" (Psalm 150, NIrV).

Preschoolers can praise God. They can listen to music, sing songs, play instruments, and move. Music activities help preschoolers worship God. They begin to understand how music is used at church to express feelings to God, to praise Him, and to thank Him. A lifetime of praising God can begin with music activities in a preschool room.

Physical

- Encourage active participation
- Facilitate the development of coordination
- Help preschoolers exercise gross motor skills through movement to music
- Enable preschoolers to exercise fine motor skills through playing instruments

Mental

- Aid in the development of auditory discrimination
- Foster creativity
- Encourage a preschooler's ability to follow directions
- Help preschoolers begin to recognize rhythms and patterns
- Allow preschoolers to create an appreciation for music

Social/Emotional

- Help preschoolers learn to take turns
- Provide opportunities for preschoolers to work together
- Can calm or stimulate preschoolers
- Allow preschoolers to experience wonder and joy
- Encourage preschoolers to express a variety of emotions

Spiritual

- Reinforce Bible truths and concepts
- Nurture a child's feelings of well-being and personal worth
- Help preschoolers worship God and talk to God
- Allow preschoolers to express their feelings about God

What Is a Music Activity?

Listening. From the youngest ages, preschoolers are listening. They listen to the voices and sounds around them. They hear music and songs from people and toys. They may not understand the words; but they develop feelings of love, acceptance, and joy through the music they hear. Middle and older preschoolers can begin to recognize familiar songs and sing them. They can differentiate between sounds and play sound-matching games. They also have emotional responses to the music they hear. They can listen to music and draw or move according to how the music makes them feel. Teachers can encourage preschoolers to listen and tell what sounds they hear; listen and repeat a pattern; or listen and tell which sounds are low and which are high.

Singing. Some children pick up and sing a song readily; others are able to sing the words but not match the tune. Musical appreciation is the goal rather than musical accuracy. Teachers should develop an atmosphere that encourages spontaneous singing. Teachers sing naturally about what the children are doing. A child sings a lullaby as she rocks the doll or builds with blocks. A preschool song is written in a middle range and contains repeated musical phrases. The song should have continuing appeal to preschoolers, even after being sung countless times. Often a preschool song lends itself to adaptation, with phrases that teachers can easily substitute to create numerous stanzas. Teachers can create fun preschool songs by using familiar tunes with new words (see p. 94). Sing songs repeatedly so preschoolers can learn them and relate them to their play. Singing (and all music activities) should help a child learn concepts and experience feelings of joy. Drilling for perfection in performance does not create enjoyment and may, in fact, create negative feelings toward music and singing.

Moving. Preschoolers are naturally active. Moving to music channels the natural energies of a child. Movement activities encourage creativity and imagination, as well as provide exercise and develop muscles. Some movement activities reinforce the rhythm and beat of the music—clapping, marching, or walking in time with the music. Other movement activities encourage children to interpret the mood of the music—bending, twisting, swaying, reaching, extending, or stretching. Children can move as the music makes them feel or can move like something else (flutter like a butterfly, sway like the wind, or lumber like an elephant). Streamers, scarves, or other accessories sometimes enhance movement activities.

Since most preschoolers focus on one thing at a time, use motions and movement with action songs only. The child will concentrate on his arms, legs, head, and body as he moves and will, as a result, not think about the words or meanings of the words in the song. The best songs to use for movement are songs that contain action words: "nod your head," "tap your toes," "clap your hands," and so forth. Avoid using movements when singing songs about biblical concepts. The words and the message of the song are more meaningful to the child when he is not distracted by motions.

Playing Instruments. Preschoolers of all ages enjoy creating music with instruments and other materials in the environment. Fill an empty plastic drink bottle with jingle bells and encourage a younger preschooler to shake it. Provide a variety of rhythm instruments for older preschoolers to use as they sing or listen to music. Allow an older preschooler or kindergartner to strum the Autoharp® or create songs on a xylophone. Children need spontaneous, unstructured time to explore using instruments. Demonstrate appropriate use and care of instruments. Allow children to choose instruments and trade with others as they experiment and create musical sounds. Encourage preschoolers to create instruments by the "found sounds" around them. They may create fun sounds by shaking seed packets or striking a spoon on a cookie sheet. Instruments for preschoolers must be safe—no sharp or protruding parts, no small parts that can be swallowed, one-piece construction, durable, and washable. Homemade instruments work as well as purchased ones. (Instructions for homemade instruments are included at the end of this chapter and on pages 116-117.)

When Is Music Used?

When the child arrives. Sing a song to welcome the child at the door. Choose a song that includes the child's name. Singing as the child arrives can ease the transition into the room.

When the child is involved in learning centers and activities. Music activities are integrated throughout the room and used in a variety of ways to guide and reinforce Bible teaching. Soft music played in the background creates a calm atmosphere. Twos march to a marching song. Threes, fours, and kindergartners draw as they listen to a Bible verse song. Songs and musical activities help teachers communicate biblical truths.

When children change from one activity to another. Transition times are easier with music. Teachers can sing a cleanup song as the children work. Singing a song can help children gather at the door and walk together to the playground. Music creates fun and smooth transitions between activities.

When children are involved in group-learning times. Music can be an important part of group time for threes, fours, pre-kindergartners, and kindergartners. In addition to using music to begin group time (transition), a teacher can sing a Bible verse song, sing a song to lead a prayer, lead children to play instruments, or use a movement song to release energy or provide relaxation.

When children need quiet times. Children can listen quietly to soft instrumental music as they lie on mats, quietly look at books, or enjoy a snack.

When children are preparing to leave. Playing a movement game or other open-ended musical game keeps children involved. Sing a good-bye song as the child leaves.

Some Guidelines for Using Music
(Even If You Can't Carry a Tune in a Bucket!)

• Play quiet instrumental music to set the atmosphere in your room.
• Learn songs for teaching preschoolers. Quarterly CDs are available for some of the curriculum you may use with preschoolers.
• Invite a musical guest to come to your room to play an instrument and sing.
• Record your children singing songs.
• Create a quiet area of the room for music and listening. Provide a CD player, CDs of appropriate music, a few musical instruments, and several blank tapes for children to

create recordings. Add streamers for movement.

- Sing. Sing often. Sing even if you sing off-key. Preschoolers do not care how you sing.
- Include the children's names in a song whenever possible. Be sure to use every child's name once you begin singing names in a song.
- Accept each child's individual response to music. Encourage each child's creativity.
- Sing songs that use words and concepts preschoolers can understand. Avoid songs with symbolism. Literal-minded preschoolers will misunderstand meanings of symbolic or abstract songs.
- Don't pressure preschoolers to rehearse or perform in programs. These activities create tension and distract from the enjoyment of music and its use in teaching.
- Use new words to familiar tunes. Create a song to fit what you need.

> The guest should visit occasionally, not come to the class for a designated "music time."

Songs to Familiar Tunes

Sometimes you cannot find a song that expresses what you need. You can create your own song! Use a familiar tune and sing the words you need. Sing children's names, a Bible verse or phrase, or instructions. Create a song with repetitive words and phrases. Choose a tune you know well. Change the words as necessary. Encourage preschoolers to create songs, too. Here are some sample songs to familiar tunes.

- To the tune "Row, Row, Row Your Boat," sing: "Clap, clap, clap your hands. Andrew claps his hands. Clapping, clapping, clapping, clapping. God made Andrew's hands."
- To the tune "God Is So Good," sing: "I can thank God. I can thank God. I can thank God. Thank You, God, for food."
- To the tune "Mulberry Bush," sing: "Open the Bible, what does it say? What does it say? What does it say? Open the Bible, what does it say? Jesus said, 'I love you.'"

Homemade Musical Instruments

Drums
- oatmeal containers with snap-on lids
- coffee cans with snap-on lids
- boxes

Shakers
- film canisters filled halfway with dried beans or rice; tape lids securely
- small chip cans filled halfway with aquarium gravel; tape lids; cover with contact plastic
- place dried beans or gravel on a small paper plate; staple second paper plate on top of first plate; tape around edges with masking tape

Rhythm Sticks
- wooden spoons
- newspaper rolled tightly and taped
- unsharpened pencils

Stringed Instruments
- rubber bands around a loaf pan
- shoe box with rubber bands

Bells
- jingle bells on chenille craft stem formed into a circle
- jingle bells sewn onto elastic loops
- jingle bells inside a plastic drink bottle

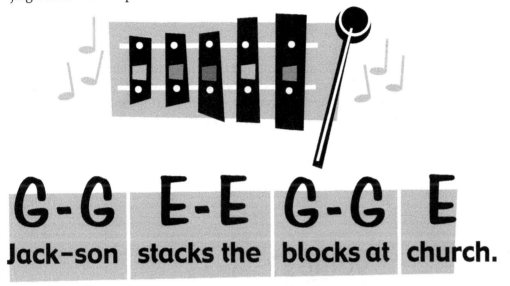

G-G   E-E   G-G   E

Jack-son   stacks the   blocks at   church.

Standardize your code on the step bells. Use these colors for the notes:

Red-C
Orange-D
Yellow-E
Green-F
Blue-G
Purple-A
Brown-B
Pink-C(high)

Music and Movement Activities

Musical Drawing—Provide paper with crayons, markers, and other drawing materials for older preschoolers. Play music and ask children to draw the way the music makes them feel. Change the music and talk about how the drawings change.

I Love a Parade—Gather instruments, flags, streamers, scarves, hats, and other materials to encourage preschoolers to form a parade. They can play and march around the room.

Create a Tune—Color-code step bells or a xylophone with a different colored sticker or paper scrap on each note. Encourage preschoolers to create their own songs. Provide markers and paper for the children to write their new songs. Add words from a Bible verse or other words to their tunes.

High and Low—Play a note on the step bells or a keyboard. Guide the children to reach up high when the note is high and squat low when the note is low.

Spontaneous Songs—Use the notes G and E to sing spontaneously about what you see the children doing. For example, sing, "Jackson stacks the blocks at church," alternating the pitch after every two syllables. Change the rhythm to fit the words.

Nature Instruments—Provide a variety of nature items for the children to use as instruments. Encourage the children to experiment with the materials to create sounds. (Include materials such as coconut shells, sticks, pebbles, and a container of water.)

Listening. Moving. Singing. Creating. Praising. Musical activities with preschoolers are an integral part of teaching biblical concepts. Early music experiences can be the beginning of a lifetime of worship and praise.

Other tunes to use:
* "Are You Sleeping?"
* "Jesus Loves Me" (chorus)
* "London Bridge"
* "Mary Had a Little Lamb"
* "Old MacDonald"
* "She'll Be Coming 'Round the Mountain"
* "Twinkle, Twinkle, Little Star"

Seeing God's Creation Through Books and Pictures

I cannot remember a time when I did not like books. My mother read to me every day from well-worn storybooks. Every night she read a Bible story from our family's favorite Bible storybook. As a child, I learned that books held words that could give me warm feelings and tell me important things. I learned that the Bible was the best book of all!

Values

Physical

- stimulate the development of eye muscles
- develop eye-hand coordination
- develop large and small muscles

Mental

- help children learn to think
- aid in problem-solving
- create awareness of print and the relationship between the written and spoken word
- encourage story writing
- help develop language and enrich vocabularies
- reinforce firsthand experiences and clarify ideas

Social / Emotional

- help children identify, understand, and respond to emotional situations
- provide time for preschoolers to be alone
- help develop an understanding of others
- create an avenue for talking about difficult and sensitive topics
- help children learn acceptable behavior
- help develop listening skills

Spiritual

- increase awareness of the world God made
- provide opportunities to see and touch the Bible
- provide opportunities to hear Bible stories and see biblical pictures
- help develop an understanding of how to live and work with others
- aid in the awareness of right and wrong

Awareness of books and print is an essential step along the path to biblical literacy. Also, an awareness of books and print is foundational for developing a love for the Bible and understanding that it is the most important book ever written. Teachers play a vital role in how children respond to books. As teachers read and share books with preschoolers, they create feelings of warmth and acceptance and lay the foundation for the love of books and reading. Books can provide opportunities for teachers to use Bible story conversation and Bible verses to create an awareness of God as Creator and Provider. For example, a book about flowers or trees provides opportunities for teachers to use the Bible phrase "God made all kinds of trees to grow" or to create a moment of awe or worship by saying: "I'm glad God made the trees for Jasmine to see. Thank You, God, for trees."

Reading books to young children should be an interactive experience. Children need opportunities to comment and discuss the story and pictures, think about what will happen next, and relate the story to their own experiences. Seeing the relevance of the words to their lives makes a book meaningful to preschoolers.

Choosing Books

When choosing books to share with preschoolers, consider books that—
- can be read in 5-10 minutes (ages 3-5)
- are written in simple language with few words to a page
- contain repetitive phrases
- have illustrations/pictures that are simple, realistic, and colorful
- picture people of different races and cultures in a positive manner
- are durable and stand the test of time
- hardcover when possible
- cardboard for young preschoolers
- homemade and paper should be laminated
- contain an interesting storyline with which the children can identify
- do not contain fantasy or cartoon characters (These are inappropriate for use in church programs. Preschoolers are unable to distinguish between fact and fantasy and may become confused if Jesus and God are presented in the same manner as fantasy characters. Avoid books with stereotyped characters and animals or objects that take on human characteristics.)

Displaying Books

Stand books in babies' cribs and on the floor near toys. Babies who are crawling and beginning to walk will enjoy books as they sit and walk. Often they will carry a favorite book around the room.

For twos through kindergartners, books can be integrated into the other Bible-learning centers and activities displayed in a book or library center. For example, as preschoolers enjoy building with blocks, a book about construction might stimulate ideas for building. Whether placed in a book center or integrated into one of the other centers, books should be displayed so that children can see the covers and easily select a book that appeals to them.

- Locate the book center near other quiet centers and away from the traffic flow.
- Display books on the floor or bookrack. Adding a colorful rug, carpet squares, or soft pillows will capture the children's interest. Create a cozy reading corner using two or three cardboard boxes.
- Change the books to reflect the session emphasis. However, the children may have favorite books that you will want to make available for several sessions.

Young preschoolers enjoy books about animals such as dogs and cats; familiar objects such as balls, blankets, and toys; and people (babies, mommies, and daddies).

Reading Books to Babies, Ones, and Twos

A child is never too young to enjoy a book. A child's love for books begins early in life, often during infancy. Preschoolers learn to love books when they are shared by a teacher who makes them feel safe and loved. Snuggle a baby on your lap and hold a book so that the baby can see the pages. Young babies will stare at books with bold black and white designs or illustrations of the human face. Older babies (8-12 months) will enjoy books with simple rhymes. They like turning the pages and looking at pictures of familiar objects.

Children soon learn that books start at the front and read from top to bottom and that the words are related to the picture. Books with one image and word per page spark a baby's interest as a teacher "reads" the pictures and relates them to the baby's world. As you read, point to the pictures and name them. Label actions and feelings. For example, say, "See the baby running." Or comment: "See the baby smiling. The baby is happy." Remember to vary the tone of your voice.

Reading Books to Threes Through Kindergartners

Books should not only be read, but also discussed. Books should be read more than once. Children understand books better when they have opportunities to ask and answer questions about the story. Children need many story-reading experiences to acquire a sense of what a story is and how it is organized. Knowing how a story begins and ends and the sequence of events is important to literacy development. Through reading experiences, children realize that stories are a means of communication. Most kindergartners can become aware that God chose to communicate to us through the stories in the Bible.

Books can be shared one-on-one, with a small group, or in large group time. To read a book to a large group, use a book with clear, colorful pictures. If there are too many words, tell the story in your own words. Hold the book facing the children so that all of them can see the pictures. Make the story come alive for the children. Point out illustrations that interest the children. Use questions to invite participation in the story. Make eye contact with each child as you read and talk. Ask them to guess what will happen next. Change your voice to match the story. Emphasize key words or phrases that are repeated, using sound effects or singing key words or phrases.

Threes through kindergartners enjoy predictable books. These books depend on predictable rhymes and rhythms that children can anticipate. Knowing what comes next encourages children to participate in the reading process.

For kindergartners, provide simple concept books. Beginning readers will be able to read these books themselves. Wordless books allow children to tell their own stories.

Books can help preschoolers deal with sensitive issues such as death, divorce, new siblings, separation, hospitalization, and fears. Books often help preschoolers replace a frightening image with a more realistic one by presenting accurate facts. In choosing books to deal with crisis situations, follow the same guidelines for choosing appropriate books, making sure that the characters and settings are those with which the children can identify and which accurately depict the situation.

Simple concept books are alphabet, number, and shape books.

Making Books

Preschoolers enjoy making books of their own. Children can dictate the text to the teacher and then draw the illustrations. Group or class books can be created in which each child has his own page to write and illustrate. When books reflect the children's experiences, they take on meaning. As older preschoolers write and illustrate their own books, teachers have opportunities to relate the experience to Bible characters who wrote books in the Bible.

- Blank Books—Make blank books by stapling 8½ by 11 inch paper together with a construction paper cover. Make a smaller book by folding the pages in half. Children can use the books to draw or write whatever they wish. They also may glue pictures in the books and write or dictate a story about them.

Teachers can use the same ideas to make books for classroom use.

- Baggie Books—Cut construction paper or poster board to fit inside ziplock bags. Glue pictures or nature objects to the paper. Slide each paper into a bag. Stack four bags together. Place the open edge of the bag at the top. Punch holes on the left side and tie the bags together with yarn or a brightly colored shoestring. Secure the tops of the bags with plastic tape when using this type of book with babies and ones.

- Big Books—Create a big book by cutting poster board into 14-by-18-inch pieces. Once a topic or theme of the book is decided, children can write or dictate a sentence and then illustrate their words. Large pieces of construction paper (12 by 18 inches) also can be used for making big books.

Pictures should be displayed at child's eye level.

Values of Pictures

- Provide the opportunity to recognize things that are familiar.
- Allow children to identify with situations common to their experiences.
- Stimulate conversation which gives teachers opportunities to gain insight into the child's thinking.
- Stimulate children's curiosity.
- Provide opportunities for worship as children look at pictures of things God made.
- Encourage children to use their imaginations to create original stories.

Choosing Pictures

Two kinds of pictures are used with preschoolers: biblical or Bible story pictures and present-day pictures. Biblical pictures portray Bible stories and scenes on the child's level of understanding. Teachers use present-day pictures to translate biblical truths into the everyday experiences of preschoolers.

Many of the same guidelines for evaluating illustrations in a book hold true for choosing pictures to use with preschoolers. Pictures should be realistic, have an uncluttered background, contain familiar objects, and be within a child's understanding.

Displaying Pictures

For babies, place pictures in cribs or on the floor for easy access. Mount pictures on cardboard and cover with clear contact paper or place them in picture holders. Picture holders can be made from clear contact plastic or plastic bags.

For older preschoolers, cut cardboard the size of the picture. Then cut four 6-by-4-inch construction paper rectangles for each corner. Place a rectangle diagonally across each corner, fold it over the back of the cardboard, and tape it in place. For added durability, laminate the construction paper rectangles before placing them on the holder. Slip the picture under each corner.

Where to Find Pictures

magazines	outdated leader guides and leader packs
calendars	junk mail
postcards	grocery store displays
newspapers	photographs
coupons	cereal boxes
catalogs (school supply, clothing, department store, seed and plant)	

How to File Pictures

Picture files can be created using a large cardboard box. Cover the box with colorful contact plastic. Cut pieces of cardboard to make dividers for the following subject headings: Old Testament, New Testament, Church, Family, God, Jesus, Creation, Self, Community and World.

Ways to Use Pictures

Pictures of different sizes and shapes can be used to teach biblical truths. For durability, laminate or cover pictures with clear contact plastic.

Crib Viewer—Make a clear-view envelope for use with babies who are not sitting. Take a piece of heavy, clear vinyl and make a pocket with a finished size of 7-by-10 inches. Turn back 1 inch on the top edges of the bag to form a casing. Stitch along the edge. Thread 2 pieces of 36-inch colored ribbon through the casing to create ends than can be tied on each side of the crib. Sew or glue Velcro® tabs or strips along the inside of the opening so that the bag can be securely closed. Stretch the bag across the crib, 12 inches above a baby's head, and tie securely. Place pictures or photographs inside for baby to view.

Memory Game—Make matching sets of picture cards by gluing small pictures to pieces of poster board. Use the cards to play a memory game. To make the game easier, back each set of cards with a different color of paper. Make the game more difficult by increasing the number of matching sets and backing all the pictures with the same color of paper.

Bible Story Puzzles—Mount Bible story pictures on cardboard or poster board using spray adhesive. Cut the picture into the number of pieces appropriate for your age group. To create a magnetic puzzle, glue small pieces of magnetic tape to the puzzle pieces and work the puzzle on a magnetic board or metal cookie sheet.

> Pictures are more than decorations for a room. They are important teaching tools.

> Using spray adhesive to mount pictures prevents the pictures from wrinkling.

Picture Webs—Place a Bible story or present-day picture on the floor. Encourage children to draw or dictate something they know about the picture or story on a strip of paper. Allow each child to place his strip of paper on the floor around the picture and connect it to the picture with a piece of yarn or ribbon. (This activity is more appropriate for kindergartners.)

Learning Together: Group Time

Chapter 15

Group time is the time during a session when the children and teachers come together for group learning experiences. During group time, preschoolers have opportunities to move, interact with others, and play games. Preschoolers are active learners, regardless of the size of the group. Three-year-olds through kindergartners can learn in a group-time experience. Departments or classes of one- and two-year-olds may have times during a session when two or three children participate in an activity together, but they should be free to leave and join the group at any time they choose.

Sometimes the beginning of the session is the best time for group time. This schedule works well with back-to-back teaching sessions, such as multiple Sunday Schools or music and missions education on Sunday or Wednesday evening. The transition between sessions may be smoother when the second session begins with a group time. One set of leaders can set up the room while the other leaders prepare to leave.

At other times, the end of the session may be the best time for group time. This plan allows for a smooth transition to Extended Teaching Care (ETC), outside play, lunch, or the arrival of parents. However, for kindergartners, you may find it helpful to allow time after the large group for the girls and boys to participate in small-group activities. These follow-up activities help kindergartners process and internalize the biblical concepts they encountered during group time.

Setting up for Group Time

Carefully plan the physical environment for group time. Free the area of distractions so the children can focus on the group activities. If the children are crowded or cannot see the teacher, they will respond with frustration or lose interest in the activity. Consider the following tips:
- Arrange the children in a semicircle facing the longest wall of the room and away from the door, if possible.
- Move furniture to make an area large enough for children and teachers.
- Encourage the preschoolers to sit in chairs or cross-legged on the floor.
- Arrange seating and control potential problems by separating children who tend to distract each other.
- Hold a picture or visual props at or slightly above the children's eye level.

To determine the length of group time, consider the age and attention span of the children. Generally, activities should be changed every three to five minutes.

Use the following suggestions as guidelines for the length of group time.

Three-year-olds	5 to 10 minutes
Four-year-olds	10 to 15 minutes
Five-year-olds and Kindergartners	15 to 20 minutes

Begin the year with a shorter group time and lengthen it as the children are able to focus their attention for longer periods of time. As you get to know the preschoolers in your class, you can adjust the length of group time as appropriate.

If a child lacks the maturity to sit for as long a period of time as others, provide him with a quiet alternative away from the group rather than force him to participate in group time. If a child is reluctant to come to group time, give him a task, such as carrying the Bible or game to the group-time area.

Transition

The transition to and from group time is often an unplanned and neglected part of a session. Transitions provide opportunities for children to learn to cooperate and be considerate of one another. Giving preschoolers plenty of notice that it is time for group time will allow them to finish activities and prepare to clean up. Use a song to signal cleanup time. A good guideline is to allow one minute of advance notice for each year of age. Guide children in the cleanup process by giving specific instructions. Rather than telling the children to "put everything away," say: "Jimmy, put the blocks on the shelf." When cleanup is almost complete, move to the group-time area and begin an activity when the first child arrives. A familiar song, finger play, or game is a good beginning activity.

Elements of Group Time

The secret to a successful group time is a well-prepared teacher who has planned a variety of activities. An unprepared teacher can quickly lose the attention and interest of the children. The teacher must know the Bible story, have all necessary visuals such as pictures or games, and know songs and finger plays. Remember that young children enjoy and need repetition, so use familiar songs, finger plays, and games.

Conversation—Preschoolers need opportunities to talk about what they have experienced during the session. Listen carefully and express genuine interest in what the children are saying. Opportunities for expressing likes, dislikes, and feelings enhance the feeling of fellowship or community among the children.

Music—Group time offers many opportunities for music. Preschoolers love songs that draw them in through actions and fun words. A teacher may choose one to two fun songs and then move to songs that relate to the session or biblical truth. Bible verse songs, Bible concept songs, or a unit song create an environment that leads to the Bible story. The addition of instruments can further create enjoyment and worship. Avoid using action songs immediately before the story. Choose songs that prepare the way for settling and listening.

Games—Incorporate games into group time for relaxation or reinforcing the Bible story or Bible verses. Play a game at the beginning of group time to encourage children to join the group. Use a game at the end of group time to keep children's attention as parents arrive.

Pictures—Use pictures to illustrate a song or Bible story. A picture helps children understand unfamiliar words. In the story of Jesus and the woman at the "well," for example, a picture of a Bible times well can help preschoolers understand the meaning of the word *well*. Ask a child to hold the picture for the group to see or pass the picture around the group. Also use pictures for games such as matching a Bible verses to a picture.

Prayer—Encourage children to pray naturally, spontaneously, and in their own words; but do not force a child to pray. Prayers of thanksgiving and praise are natural responses for children. As children grow and develop, they may begin to express other types of prayers as well. Kindergartners may express prayers such as, "Help me be kind to my friends." Help preschoolers begin to understand they can pray anytime, anywhere, about anything. As you pray with preschoolers, remember these guidelines:

- Begin the prayer with a simple address to God.
- Use simple phrases and avoid symbolic words like God's Word or God's House.
- Do not force children to bow their heads and close their eyes. Focus on the practice and purpose of prayer rather than the position of prayer. Preschoolers need to see prayer that is purposeful and spontaneous.
- Allow children to talk to God in a natural way rather than recite a memorized prayer. Preschoolers need to see and hear adults talking to God in understandable and natural ways.
- Use the names of preschoolers in the prayer.
- Use a large sheet of paper to list the children's prayer requests.

Bible—Use a Bible designed for preschoolers throughout the group-time experience. Children need opportunities to touch and look at the Bible. Prior to the session, highlight Bible verses in the Bible. Make simple Bible markers by cutting two-inch strips of colored paper and printing a Bible verse on each strip. Place the markers in the Bible. When a child chooses a marker, repeat the Bible verse and show the words in the Bible.

Kindergartners who bring their Bibles to church may choose to use them during group time. Help the children find one of the Bible verses or the reference for the Bible story. Invite kindergartners to mark the place in their Bible with a strip of construction paper. They may enjoy looking at the picture of the story in their Bibles after the Bible story. Remember to use a Bible with realistic illustrations. Avoid using a Bible storybook instead of a Bible. Preschoolers need an accurate perception of what a Bible is. However, avoid telling a child who wants to use her own Bible that her Bible is only a storybook.

Bible Story—Storytelling, especially telling Bible stories, is an effective tool for teaching biblical truths to preschoolers. God used storytelling to give His message of redemption to people. Jesus was the Master Storyteller, using stories in His teachings. Jesus responded to the disciples' question, "Why do you tell stories?" (Matthew 13:10):

He (Jesus) replied: "You've been given insight into God's kingdom. You know how it works. Not everybody has this gift, this insight; it hasn't been given to them. Whenever someone has a ready heart for this, the insights and understandings flow freely. But if there is no readiness, any trace of receptivity soon disappears. That's why I tell stories: to create readiness, to nudge the people toward receptive insight."[1]

Telling Bible stories prepares preschoolers to receive the message of God's love. Preparing to tell the Bible story should be taken seriously. "The person who makes Bible stories come alive will be one who loves stories and wants to tell them so the lessons they teach will be printed indelibly on the minds of the listeners."[2] Effective storytelling involves an interaction between the teller (teacher), the listener (child), and the story.

Storytelling Tips and Techniques

Prepare the Story
1. Read the Bible story in several translations. Also read the passages before and after the story for context. Look up words used in the text. Having a good background for the story will make it easier to tell and remember.
2. The better you are able to picture the story in your mind, the better you can relate that story to the children. Create story boards in your mind of the sequence of the events. If you have to look back at the printed copy, you have not spent enough time preparing to tell the story. The story must become your story.
3. Story length should be about one minute for every year of the children's age.
4. Practice telling the story in front of a mirror. Record the story so you can listen to it. By listening, you are able to learn and refine the story, making it your own. The more you practice, the easier the story will flow.

Tell the Story
As you become comfortable with the Bible story, you may find that it is easy to lose yourself in the telling of the story. When you connect with the Bible story and the preschoolers, both you and the children will have a memorable experience. Use a natural and relaxed manner and an expressive tone of voice. Hold the attention of the boys and girls with your voice. Speed up, slow down. Lower your voice or raise it. Express delight and surprise, create suspense. Keep the children totally involved in the story.
1. Make eye contact with each child, remembering to sit on their level.
2. Open the Bible to the correct reference and hold the Bible on your lap.
3. Grab the children's attention with the first sentence. Get the action going.
4. Alter the timing or pace of the story. Think about how boring music or life would be if everything existed at the same speed.
5. Portray characters and events with your voice and your gestures, keeping in mind that gestures should be genuine, but not exaggerated.
6. Tools for storytelling:

Voice: Your voice is your most important tool in telling Bible stories. The tone and mood of your voice should interpret the Bible story. The feelings of fear, sadness, anger, frustration, or even sleepiness should be evident in your voice to the same degree that they are evident in the story. The speed and direction of your voice will communicate. Example: "Jeremiah was put into a hole in the ground. He went down, down, deep, deep down in the hole." Your voice can drop with the words "down" and "deep." Also, using action words and sound words ("Slap," "Crash") can add interest, movement, and meaning to the Bible story. The pitch and inflection of the voice should be used from time to time to indicate different characters in a story. Be careful. Too much character can distract from the story.

Facial Expression: Your face is the movie screen of the story. It can be blank with sound only or filled with the action of the story. A smile or a frown can help project the image of the place and people. As you portray different people in the story, think about what their faces would look like.

Gestures and Movements: The best rule for using gestures is to use only meaningful gestures and to use them on a limited basis. Storytellers who use gestures and movements for every event or person in the story risk losing the preschoolers or making gestures and movement less significant by overuse.[3]

After the Story

1. A good story does not require an interpretation. The meaning should be clear. If something needs a long explanation, it will distract from the purpose of the story and the outcome of the session. "The words I speak are like that. They will not return to me without producing results. They will accomplish what I want them to" (Isaiah 55:11, NIrV).

2. Show a picture to illustrate the story. Evaluate the preschoolers' interpretation of the story by using follow-up questions like: "How do you think Zacchaeus felt when Jesus called to him?" Questions help preschoolers begin to internalize the biblical truths.

3. Other possible follow-up activities:
• Role-play the story or a favorite part of the story.
• Picture pose using the Bible story picture.
• Divide the children into pairs and ask them to retell the story.

4. Continue to involve the children in a game or activity until parents or Extended Teaching Care (ETC) teachers arrive or until time to transition to another activity. Encourage arriving parents to knock on the door and wait for a teacher to bring the child to them. When only one or two children remain, ask them to help put away materials until their parents arrive.

Group-time Tips

1. Preschoolers are just beginning to develop social skills. Be patient.
2. Watch for signs of listening fatigue.
3. If children become restless, put more energy or expression in your voice.
4. Stopping the story to call a child back to attention is a distraction. By holding the attention of the group, many times the inattentive child becomes a listener again.
5. Avoid asking questions during the story.

6. Do not disrupt the flow of a story by stopping to define a word. Children like words and can understand the meaning in the greater context of the story. However, you can clarify the meaning by using conversational remarks. For example, to explain the word *tabernacle*, say: "Moses asked the people to give special offerings for the tabernacle God wanted them to build. The tabernacle was a special tent church."

Games and Activities

Songs or Chants
Sing the following to the tune "Happy Birthday":
"Good morning to you. Good morning to you. Good morning to (*child's name*). How do you do?"

Sing the following to the tune "The Farmer in the Dell":
"We're all here today. (*Clap hands as you sing.*) We're all here today. Let's all clap together, Because we're here today."

"(*First child's name*) is here today. (*Second child's name*) is here today. (*Third child's name*) is here today. And (*fourth child's name*) is here today."

Continue singing until all the children are mentioned.

Games
Play Copycat—Use different volumes with your voice as you say, "If you can hear me, do what I'm doing."
Mirror Game—As children come to group time, hand the first child an unbreakable hand mirror and sing the following song to the tune "Are You Sleeping?": "You are special. You are special. Take a look. You will see. Someone very special. Someone very special. It is you! It is you!"
Mystery Box—Cover a shoe box with colorful contact plastic. Place a nature object, book, or item relating to the session's focus inside the box. Tie a colorful ribbon around the box. During group time, pass the box around the group and allow the children to ask questions about what is in the box. After everyone has had a turn to guess what is in the box, open it and remove the item.

Bible Games
Hide and Seek Bible Verses—Print a Bible verse on a paper strip. Cut apart the strip so each word is separate. Tape each word onto a wooden block. Hide the blocks around the room and encourage the girls and boys to find them. Comment, "When you find one block, come sit with me." When all the blocks are found, guide the children to place them in a line so that they form the Bible verse. Variation for older preschoolers: Ask children to stack the blocks so that you can read the verse from bottom to top.
Hot Potato Bible Verse—Insert the Bible markers in the Bible. The preschoolers sit in a circle with the Bible in the center. Pass a beanbag or small ball around the circle as you play a cassette tape or CD of music. Stop the music. Encourage the child holding the beanbag or ball to open the Bible to a marker. Read the Bible verse aloud. Resume play.
Search for a Bible Character—Print on cards the letters in the name of one of the session's Bible story characters. Hide the cards. Children search for the cards as they come to group time. When a child finds a card, he comes to the circle. When all the cards are found, arrange them to spell the name. Then tell the Bible story.

Bible Concept Games

I Have Friends at Church—Children sit in a circle on the floor. One child walks around the outside of the circle. To the tune "Mary Had a Little Lamb," sing: "Davis came to church today, church today, church today. Davis came to church today. Now he can pick a friend." (*Use the child's name in the song.*) When Davis touches a friend, the friend stands and walks around the circle as you sing. Davis sits where his friend was sitting. Continue playing until every child has a turn to walk around the circle and pick a friend.

God Loves Us—Locate a ball or a beanbag. Stand with the children in a circle. Ask, "Whom does God love?" As you roll or toss the ball to a child, answer, "God loves (*child's name*)." The child you name catches the ball and says, "God loves (*child's name*)" as he throws the ball to another child. Continue until each child has a turn.

I Can Say Thank You to God—Say, "I thank God for something that is blue." Encourage the children to name blue items in the room until a child guesses the item you had in mind. The child who guesses correctly then says, "I thank God for something that is (*name the color*)." Play until each child has had a turn.

Bible Phrase Games

1. Invite a child to select a marker from the Bible and place it on an appropriate picture. Or whisper the verse to him and let him tell others.
2. Print Bible verses on different colored strips of construction paper and cut in two parts. Distribute the pieces and let the children match colors.
3. Toss a beanbag or non-bouncing fun ball onto a gameboard made of four colored sheets of construction paper. Ask the child to find a Bible marker or picture with the same color.
4. Print each word of a Bible verse on a large craft stick. Place the sticks in a colorful bag or can. Invite children to choose a stick. Guide the children to place the words in order.

[1] Eugene H. Peterson, *THE MESSAGE: The New Testament Psalms and Proverbs* (Colorado Springs: NavPress, 1995), 29.
[2] Maxine Bersch, *Storytelling in a Nutshell* (Nashville: LifeWay Press, 1998), 124.
[3] Adapted from The National Storytelling Association, *Tales as Tools* (Jonesborough: National Storytelling Press, 1994), 88.

Playing Inside and Out

"Let's race. No, let's play firehouse!" Indoors or outdoors, children love to play games. Whether those games are part of cooperative play or free play, preschoolers find ways to create their own imaginative games.

Preschoolers need time to be free to run, jump, climb, and explore. Free play allows preschoolers to release energy. In the process, they also stimulate their minds, exercise their bodies, draw other preschoolers into their games, make choices, and develop a healthy self-concept through acting out their inner feelings.

Physical

- Develops fine motor skills and eye-hand coordination
- Develops gross motor skills and eye-foot coordination
- Aids in coordination and agility
- Strengthens bones and muscles
- Teaches body awareness

Mental

- Develops self-concept
- Encourages creativity
- Develops mental awareness
- Encourages feelings of adequacy and happiness
- Aids in the learning of sequencing, patterning, and numbering
- Develops recall skills

Social / Emotional

- Develops healthy self-worth
- Releases tension
- Aids in feelings of belonging and security
- Teaches cooperation and respect for others
- Teaches spatial awareness
- Strengthens group participation
- Teaches rules
- Develops decision-making skills

Spiritual

- Develops appreciation for God's creation
- Shows respect for God, self, and others
- Creates feelings of trust and security
- Allows choices

As weather permits, preschoolers need time to explore the outdoors. Use your imagination when creating a stimulating learning environment on the playground. Some things to consider when designing this environment are:

• Available space for play area;
• Ages of children who will use the play space;
• Approaches through which the children learn (physical, logical, verbal, reflective, relational, musical, natural, and visual);
• Hygiene and safety issues such as covered sandboxes, water sources, and age-suitable equipment;

Playground Learning Centers

Active play: Include slides, climbers, platforms, walkways, and a grassy area for group games with hoops, balls, or parachutes.
Sand play: Include a sandbox or digging area with small, safe, digging tools.
Water play: Include a water table or dishpans of water with a variety of water toys (plastic bowls, cups, spoons, funnels, and turkey basters).
Dramatic play: Provide easy-to-carry prop boxes with dress-up clothes, plastic washable hats, and washable toys to enhance and enrich imaginative play.
Quiet play: Provide a bench or low crawl space where children can rest and be quiet or where children can read a book with the teacher.
Science and Nature play: Include a small area for a seasonal garden, bird houses and feeders, a small petting area for a visiting pet, and a grassy area for bubble play.
Art play: Provide a small plastic easel or child-sized table where children can be creative with a variety of art materials.
Riding trail: Provide an enclosed patio or riding trail for riding toys such as tricycles.

Playground Design and Safety

As you design your outdoor space, give safety top priority. The top causes of injury on a playground are inadequate supervision, improper protective surfaces, inappropriate equipment, lack of proper maintenance of equipment, and improper spacing of equipment. The U. S. Consumer Product Safety Commission suggests the following safety guidelines for providing a safe playground.

• Equipment is free of splinters, pinch points, and sharp edges.
• Stationary equipment is anchored securely into the ground at proper depths, depending on the height of the equipment.
• Horizontal guardrail openings are no greater than 9 inches.
• Platforms 20 inches or higher require guardrails.
• Space between steps and ladders has a distance of less than 12 inches.
• Guardrail heights are at least 30 inches high for preschool children.
• Platforms of freestanding slides are 29 inches long.

"God gives us things to enjoy" (1 Timothy 6:17).

- Swings are attached with closed O-rings and not open S-hooks.
- There are no more than two swings per bay.
- Fall zones in front and behind swings are twice the height of the swing.
- Balance beams are 9 inches or less in height.
- Adequate fall zones all equipment are provided.
- Ground below equipment is covered with 12 inches of impact-absorbing surface materials such as shredded rubber tires, mats, pea gravel, sand, or mulch. Pre-mats or molded surfaces may vary in height depending on the absorbency of the material.

Safety Tip: Develop a playground safety checklist. Plan monthly or bi-monthly inspections. The checklist should include:

___ Stationary equipment is secure.
___ Bolts are secure.
___ Sharp edges are covered.
___ O-rings on swings are secure.
___ Sandbox and water table are securely covered.
___ Impact-absorbing surface is at proper depth for equipment.
___ Wood is splinter free.
___ Playground is free of standing water.
___ Playground is free of debris.
___ Tree roots are covered.
___ Riding trail is even and free of dangerous holes.

> "Help one another"
> (Galatians 5:13).

Simple Rules for Safe Play on the Playground

As you set safety rules for the playground, remember that the simpler the rule, the easier it is to remember and enforce. Priority rules are those that protect preschoolers from getting hurt or hurting someone else. Here are some examples of simple rules for playground safety.

- Two adults must be present at all times when children are on the playground.
- One person is allowed on the slide at a time.
- Face forward when sliding down the slide.
- Do not stand on the slide.
- Only one person per swing is allowed.
- Do not twist and untwist when on the swing.
- Sit in the center of the swing.
- Never swing empty swings.
- Do not jump off platforms over 18 inches high.
- One person at a time is allowed on the climber.
- Never play rough on the equipment.
- Throwing sand or running with sticks is never allowed.

Safety Tip

For more information on playground safety and a free guide, go to CPSC.gov.

Using Games and Recreational Activities with Preschoolers

Stages of Play

Independent play—Infants through young twos play alone. As you watch younger preschoolers in the same class, each child seems to be playing in his own world. Interaction with other preschoolers is limited to protecting their territory.

Parallel play—Preschoolers around 18 months through older twos begin playing with occasional interaction with other children. Watch as young preschoolers play in the sandbox and observe how they interact with each other. At this stage children appear to be playing with each other, but their conversation shows that each child is involved in her own world. Look for games that allow the child to work alone such as running or hopping. Sing the instructions to a familiar tune such as "Ring Around the Rosie."

Partner Play—Three-year-olds begin looking for a partner with whom to play. They may begin participating in simple group games. Children may be impatient waiting for turns. Consider games that pair children or put them in small groups such as catching a beanbag or ball.

Group play—Older preschoolers begin to feel more comfortable playing in a larger group. Even though the children begin to work together more, they still have a hard time waiting for their turns. Remember that games need to strengthen the concept of working together. Avoid competitive games. Games that allow children to each have a turn, use numbers, or move to music are excellent choices for this age. The game "Doorways" below is a good example.

Doorways (ages 3 to 8)—Instruct the children to form a circle and join hands to form "doors." Choose a child to be "It" and stand in the middle of the circle. Tell the child to repeat this verse:

"I want to go out to play.
I want to go out to play.
Please open the door.
So I can go out to play."

When she finishes, the other children raise their arms to open the doors. The child runs into and out of the doors as the other children count to 10. When they reach 10, the children let down their arms to close the doors. If the child is inside the circle, she is "It" again. If she is outside the circle, she chooses a friend to become "It." Continue until every child has a turn.

Cooperative Games vs. Competitive Games

No one likes to lose. Competitive games with preschoolers often result in hurt feelings or a lack of desire to try the game again. These games may affect a child's self-concept or even her feelings about church. Reflective and logical learners may even refuse to participate in any group games that result in one side winning and another losing. Using competitive games may cause the less physical child to refrain from participating in any game. One goal of using games is to set a foundation for a healthy, active lifestyle.

Using cooperative games with older preschoolers teaches children to work together, respect others, learn to share space, observe rules, and develop decision-making skills. In cooperative games everyone wins, and children experience success rather than failure. Cooperative games such as "Follow the Leader" begin laying a foundation of team building by teaching the children how to work toward a common goal.

Planning Games for Preschoolers

As you begin planning games for preschoolers, one of the first things to consider is where you will be playing. Remember to look for a large grassy space free of holes, roots, and rocks. Consider weather conditions as you plan for outdoor games. Games may be harder to play if the grass is wet or if children are bundled up because it is too cold.

When planning to play games inside, remember space is important. Look for a room or gym that is free of all other equipment. Look for carpeted space that will cushion falls. Gyms have great open spaces, but use caution on the slick surface.

Playing Inside and Out

Other things to consider when planning games are:

1. Use simple movement activities that encourage jumping, running, and hopping.
2. Choose games that allow the children to imitate the adult leader.
3. Participate with the children.
4. Know the instructions for the games.
5. Gather all the equipment before you begin the game.
6. Give simple instructions. The younger the child, the simpler the instructions.
7. Demonstrate the game for the visual learner; sing the instructions for the musical learner.
8. Repeat the instructions as often as needed.
9. Teach the game in parts. For example, teach children how to roll the ball. Next, give each child a number. Pass the ball around while each child repeats his number. Then, pass the ball calling out random numbers.
10. Repeat the game several times so children will become familiar with the game.
11. Encourage children to suggest different ways to play the game.
12. Quit before the children get bored with the game.

Movement and cooperative playtime for preschoolers needs to contain certain elements. These elements are warm-up time, games, and wind-down time. Warm-up time includes activities such as movement to music and passing the ball. These activities are intended to stretch and limber up muscles. Wind-down time, or transition time, includes activities that are intended to help preschoolers calm down. Activities include guessing games, slow action songs, or finger plays.

Equipment

Many games used with preschoolers such as "Duck, Duck, Goose" do not require equipment. Yet, simple equipment can enhance or change an old game into a new one. For example, play "Duck, Duck, Goose" with a parachute. Guide the children to move the parachute up and down. The child who is "It" walks around saying, "Duck, duck, duck, and goose." When the child picks a goose, instead of running around the outside of the circle, the two children run around the circle under the parachute.

Balls—Find a variety of shapes and sizes. Since preschoolers enjoy balls, look for light, soft-sided balls such as beach balls.

Hoops—Gather large plastic hoops.

Parachute—Purchase parachutes in several sizes (6 to 12 feet). You can make a small parachute by cutting a king-sized flat sheet into a circle.

Scarves—Use scarves in movement activities.

Ropes—Use ropes in games with older preschoolers. Supervise closely when using them.

Playing Games with Multiple Age Groups

One of the greatest benefits of playing games in multiple age group settings is that younger preschoolers can learn from older preschoolers. Be sure that teams have equal numbers of each age group. For example, if there are 6 kindergartners, 5 fours, and 7 threes, then each team would have 3 kindergartners, at least 2 fours, and at least 3 threes. Remember that close supervision and interaction with adults is necessary. Also, when forming teams, adult leaders should choose the teams.

Simple games are fun for the children and teachers. As adults interact with preschoolers, they begin to develop stronger relationships with each other. Teachers can encourage children to learn patience as they patiently teach games to the children.

> "We work together" (1 Corinthians 3:9).

113

Finding a Place for All That Stuff

aybe you've heard in the hallway. Maybe you've said it yourself. "We don't have the money to buy all that stuff to use at church with preschoolers. How are we supposed to teach if we don't have the resources?" Teaching preschoolers takes stuff, and sometimes you don't have all the stuff. You don't have it; you can't get it; and you don't know what to do about it.

You don't need to have every single suggested item to teach preschoolers. In fact, you can have too much stuff. While preschoolers need choices, offering too many choices can be overstimulating. A cluttered room will not be the best the learning environment. Preschoolers need space to move and learn. Sometimes fewer resources provide the spark for preschoolers to launch their creativity.

However, you can have too little. If you have only three crayons and a couple of blocks, then you need to add to your resources. With a little ingenuity, you can come up with the resources without squeezing every last dime from the budget. Resources don't have to be purchased from a store.

1. Reuse—Often, items that can be used by preschoolers are collecting dust in garages, basements, or attics. Publicize the need for toys and other resources and encourage church members to donate safe, usable items. You also may also find inexpensive items at garage sales (or similar sales).

Use the following questions to determine if an item is suitable to use:
• Is the toy suitable for the age group? Toys may be appropriate for older preschoolers but dangerous for babies, ones, and twos.
• Is the toy free of sharp edges, points, or small parts that can be swallowed?
• Is the toy made of nonflammable, nontoxic, lead-free materials?
• Is the toy washable? Can it be cleaned easily in the room? Avoid stuffed animals and other fabric toys since they cannot be easily cleaned each week.
• Can the toy withstand frequent use by a group of children?
• Is the toy appropriate for use in a group setting?
• Can the toy be used in a variety of creative ways?
• Will the toy provide natural opportunities for Bible teaching and learning?

2. Request—You can obtain new materials at no cost through donations. Some churches have a "preschool shower" so church members can donate materials to the preschool ministry. Needs are publicized so individuals or groups can purchase items. When listing needs, be specific by listing toy and manufacturer so you receive what you need. People unfamiliar with the needs of preschoolers may purchase a toy that is not suitable for church use.

3. Recycle—Can't buy it? Can't find it? Make it! You can use recycled materials to create toys for preschoolers. In fact, preschoolers often play with teacher-made resources more than purchased materials. After all, haven't you seen a child ignore the toy and play with the box? You can turn the box into a toy!

Making resources for preschoolers does not require a great deal of time, expense, or expertise. Often the resources can be made in minutes after assembling the necessary supplies. While some preschool resources may need a hammer and nails, or needle and thread, most are easy to make with materials that are easy to find. Most materials are around your house. And remember, even teacher-made items must pass the above usability questions.

Gather these basic tools to create a "tool box" for making preschool resources.
• Scissors and utility knife
• Spray adhesive or glue
• Clear contact plastic and colored contact plastic
• Adhesive remover (for removing labels, and so forth)
• Masking tape, clear tape

Teacher-made Art Materials

Stickers—Mix 2 parts white glue and 1 part white vinegar. Add a drop of flavoring if desired. Apply the mixture to the back of small pictures. Let dry. Apply mixture again and let dry. Store until ready to use. When ready to use, moisten back of picture and press to the desired surface.

Play Dough—Mix 1 cup flour, ½ cup salt, and 2 teaspoons cream of tartar in a bowl. In a separate container, mix 1 cup water, 1 tablespoon cooking oil, and food color as desired. Pour both mixtures into an electric skillet heated to medium heat. Keep stirring until mixture begins to pull away from the pan and becomes doughy. Remove dough from the pan and knead until smooth. Store dough in an airtight container. Avoid using dough more than one for hygiene purposes.

Collage Box—Cut tops from four clean, half-gallon milk cartons. Tape cartons together with open ends facing the same way. Cover sides with colorful contact plastic. Put different collage materials in each section. This box can also be used for a sorting game.

Teacher-made Dramatic Play/Homeliving Materials

Chef Hat—Cut a poster board strip long enough to fit around a child's head. Staple the strip into a ring. Insert a small white paper bag inside the ring and staple around outside edge until the bag is firmly attached. As an alternative, staple a piece of white cloth or paper to the inside of the ring to create the shape of a chef's hat. Cover the staples with masking tape.

Medical Kit—Locate an old purse or gym bag. Inside the "medical bag," place an old white shirt and a pair of eyeglass frames (lenses removed). Gather a mini flashlight, cotton balls, an ice pack, washcloths, and masking tape strips on waxed paper (for adhesive bandages). Also, add cloth strips for bandages and slings. Use earphones from a personal cassette player to serve as a stethoscope. (Attach felt circles to the plug.) Remember to add a notepad and pencil.

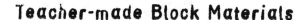

Teacher-made Block Materials

Velcro® Blocks—Gather several small boxes, such as cornbread mix boxes. Stuff the boxes with newspaper. Cover the boxes with colored contact plastic. Cut strips of sticky-backed Velcro fastener. Attach pieces of fastener to the box top and bottoms. Children can stick the boxes together and pull them apart.

Pull Toy—Cover a shoe box or other box with colored contact plastic, if desired. Punch two holes in one end of the box and attach one plastic chain link (from a linking set) through the box. Attach additional links to the first link to make a "pull string." Place an item of interest in the box. (Note: Yarn may be used instead of links for a pull string. Cut yarn no longer than 12 inches. Securely attach a large bead or plastic bracelet to the end to a grip.)

Teacher-made Puzzles and Manipulatives Materials

Lock Board—Sand the edges of an 18-inch piece of plywood. Cover rough edges with colored cloth tape or vinyl tape. Screw several types of locks, latches, or bolts into the board. Cover screw heads with cloth tape or vinyl tape.

Box-Front Puzzles—Cut the front from cereal boxes and boxes of other food products. Cut the cover into several pieces (fewer pieces for younger preschoolers and more pieces for older preschoolers). Add magnetic tape to the back of each piece. Children can work puzzles on a metal pan or tray.

Color Sorter—Gather a utensil tray and colored craft sticks. Children can sort the different colors in the compartments. Younger preschoolers can fill-and-dump the tray.

Teacher-made Nature and Science Materials

Bubble Solution—In a plastic bowl mix ½ cup water, 4 tablespoons dishwashing detergent, and 1½ tablespoons light corn syrup. Remove the ends from a soup can (cover edges with masking tape) or collect empty thread spools. Dip cone end of the can or spool in the bubble solution and blow gently to make bubbles.

Plastic Apron (for water play)—From a plastic tablecloth or shower curtain, cut a rectangle that measures 36 inches long and 15 inches wide. Cut a neck opening in the center of the rectangle that measures about 10 inches wide. Cut a 36-inch-long sash from the tablecloth or shower curtain to tie around the child's waist to secure the apron.

Insect Bottle—Cut off the top of a 2-liter drink bottle. Place a butterfly or other insect inside the bottle. Slide the open end of the bottle into a clean nylon stocking and tie the stocking end into a knot. Cut off any excess stocking.

Rolling Toy—Cut the tops from two 2-liter drink bottles (where they begin to narrow). Inside one bottle, place nature items (such as leaves) or colorful foam shapes. Slide the open end of the filled bottle into the empty bottle. Wrap wide transparent tape around the exposed cut edge to secure the bottles. Roll toy toward a baby or younger preschooler.

Teacher-made Music Materials

Clackers—To make simple clackers, tie two metal teaspoons or tablespoons together with a short piece of yarn. Invite a child to hold the yarn and clink the spoons together.

Moving Streamers—Locate a travel toothbrush case. Open the case into two pieces. (One toothbrush case will make two streamers.) Cut several strands of different colors, narrow gift wrap ribbon. Thread the strands through the hole in the end of the toothbrush case. Pull the strands through the toothbrush case until you can grab the ends at the large opening. Tie the strands into a large knot at one end to join the strands together. Pull the knot back inside the toothbrush case until the knot lodges inside the hole at the end of the case. A child can grasp the plastic case for a handle and move the streamers to music.

Teacher-made Books and Picture Materials

Peek-and-Find Picture—Cut two 10-by-12-inch pieces of cardboard. In the center of one piece, draw a rectangle that is two inches smaller than the piece of cardboard. Use a utility knife to make a flap by cutting down the sides and across the bottom of the smaller rectangle. Do not cut the top of the rectangle. Lay this piece of cardboard on top of the second piece. Tape the bottoms and the sides of the cardboard pieces together, leaving the top free. You may want to place colored masking tape down the two sides and bottom to finish off the edges. Slide a teaching picture into the slot in the top. Preschoolers can lift the flap and to discover the biblical picture. Note: You may need to use a utility knife to cut a notch at the top center of the back piece of cardboard for easy removal of the picture.

Picture Roll—Cover a cylindrical salt container with brown wrapping paper. Mount small pictures of families (or other theme) on the sides of the container. (Spray adhesive works well.) Cover the mounted pictures with clear contact plastic. A baby can crawl after the rolling toy and look at the pictures.

Teacher-made Group-time Materials

Beanbag—Cut two rectangles of fabric that measure 4 inches by 6 inches. Sew the two rectangles together, right sides together, with an ½-inch seam, leaving a small opening on one end. Double stitch the beanbag for durability. Turn the bag inside out and stuff the beanbag. You can stuff beanbags with foam packing peanuts, small plastic pellets, beans, cotton batting, or panty hose. Hand stitch the opening closed.

Bible Verse Game—Place squares of different colors in a paper bag. Place markers of matching colors in the Bible. A child pulls a square from the bag and chooses the matching Bible marker.

Teacher-made Playground Materials

Wind Streamers—Cut a narrow strip of crepe paper or colorful ribbon. Tape to the tips of a large craft stick. Allow to dry. Invite a preschooler to hold the craft stick and move his streamer in the wind.

Large Play Mat—Sew two vinyl tablecloths together around the edges. Leave a 2-foot opening. Stuff the tablecloths with old sheets and soft fabrics. (Remove any buttons and sharp objects from worn clothing before stuffing the mat.) Sew the opening shut.

From This to That

Many things around your house are just waiting to be used for preschool Bible teaching. These lists can get your creative juices flowing. Look for the things around your house. Can you use them to involve boys and girls in learning about God and the Bible?

 Ways to Use a Ziplock Bag
- Finger Paint (Place two colors of paint inside bag and seal; guide child to press on outside to mix colors.)
- Terrarium (Dip a few cotton balls in water and drop them in the bag; sprinkle grass seed on cotton balls; seal bag and tape to window.)
- Mini First Aid Kit for emergencies (include adhesive bandage strips, cotton balls, antibacterial ointment)

 Ways to Use a Cardboard Box
- Car Tunnel (Cut ends off shoe box and turn box upside down.)
- Fill-and-Dump Toy (Cut large horizontal slot in lid of shoe box; put lid on box; place box on floor with several small plastic lids; child can push lids through slot and open shoe box to recover them.)
- Doll Bed (Cover shoe box with colored contact plastic, if desired; fold towel or blanket in the bottom for a mattress; lay doll and small blanket on top.)

 Ways to Use a Cardboard Tube
- Sorting Game (Tubes of assorted lengths.)
- Whisper Tube (Hold one end of tube near child's ear; whisper message.)
- Cookie Cutter (Children can cut circle "cookies" in play dough.)
- Ball Tunnel (Cover a gift wrap tube with colored contact plastic; use with tennis ball.)

 Ways to Use a Muffin Pan
- matching game (place small matching items in sections; cover with lids)
- sorting game (provide older preschoolers with a bag with items to sort; use varieties of beans or pasta, buttons, beads, or other small items)

Alternative to Furnishings and Equipment

Sometimes, you have the teaching resources, toys, or materials you need. What you lack are furnishings or other larger equipment. Creativity is the key to a successful teaching-learning environment. Use this chart to kick-start your ideas:

Instead of	*Use*
Easel	Plastic drop cloth taped to wall
Easel	Appliance box with top cut off
Parachute (for group games)	Large flat sheet
Wooden people figures	Pictures cut from catalog
Table	Cafeteria trays on the floor
Table	Large box turned bottom side up
Chairs	Carpet squares (carpet samples)
Tent	Sheet draped over a table or chairs
Beanbag	Socks folded into a ball
Instant-print camera and film	Crayons and paper for self portraits
Shelves	Two cardboard boxes glued one on top of the other (open ends facing to the side)
Stove	Cardboard box (24 by 12 by 18 inches); draw on burners, door, knobs
Sink	Cardboard box (24 by 12 by 18 inches); cut hole in top for dishpan

Recyclable Materials to Gather

Aerosol can tops
Aluminum pie pans
Brads
Buttons
Cardboard pieces

Cardboard tubes (short and lone
Carpet samples
Clothespins (spring and peg types)
Coat hangers (plastic)
Coffee cans
Construction paper and scraps
Cookie cutters
Craft sticks, tongue depressors
Crayons, crayon pieces
Dishcloths, plastic dish scrubbers
Dishpan
Dowels
Egg cartons
Elastic
Fabric scraps, felt scraps
Film canisters (35mm)
Foam trays (new, not recycled)
Food containers (empty)
Frozen dinner trays
Funnels
Glue, glue sticks
Greeting cards (no fantasy characters)
Hole punch

Keys, key chains
Kitchen utensils (safe)
Magazines, catalogs
Margarine tubs
Masking tape (regular and colored)
Mesh bags
Milk cartons
Muffin pans
Nature items from local area
Newspapers
Oatmeal boxes
Paper bags
Paper plates
Paper muffin cups
Plastic drink bottles
Postcards
Poster board (white, colored)
Purses, wallets
Ribbon, lace, rickrack, trims
Rubber bands
Sand
Sandpaper
Spools, thread cones
Spray bottles
Tablecloths
Wooden spoons
Yarn, string
Ziplock bags (all sizes)

Getting a Handle on All Your Resources

You're feeling better about your resources. You've inventoried what you have. You have purchased some new and used toys. You have received donations from church members to fill in the gaps. You have gathered recyclable materials and made some resources. Now what are you going to do with all that stuff?

Many churches designate a central place for storing preschool resources. Maybe your church needs a resource room or supply closet. Some churches have more than one location for storing items—a resource room for more permanent items (puzzles, books, musical instruments, nature items) and a supply room for consumable items (construction paper, paint, shoe boxes). Other churches have one location for all items. However you decide to organize the resources, the key is organization.

Wooden Puzzles—Wooden puzzles are stored most easily by being stacked. Narrow divided shelves keep stacks manageable. Print the name of the puzzle and number of pieces on the edge with a permanent marker. Stack the puzzles alphabetically by name. Teachers can scan the shelves quickly to find the puzzle they need.
Books—Stand books on shelves with bookends. Sort the books by subject area, alphabetically by author, or alphabetically by title. If you use an alphabetical system,

create a book list by subject area for teacher reference. (This system works well if books can be used in more than one subject area.) Keep a computerized list or maintain a subject list on index cards in a card file. Shelve books from kits or leader packs with other purchased books.

Music Resources—Stand cassette tapes and compact discs with titles showing. Create a reference file of songs and the tape or CD on which the song is recorded. Keep the song list in a notebook and update it frequently.

Other Resources—Other types of resources can be stored in containers on shelves. Label each container and each shelf so that everyone will know what belongs where. You may also want to number the shelves and create an index for reference and easy location of supplies. Consider these ideas for storing materials and supplies:

• Plastic crates, baskets, and dishpans can be used for most items.
• Transparent storage boxes with lids and shoe boxes can store smaller items.
• Ziplock bags placed in a larger storage container can hold small game pieces or other items.
• Cans with lids or oatmeal boxes with lids can hold felt-tip markers.
• Plastic frosting containers with lids are good containers for crayons. Place sets of crayons in one container or store by color (if you purchase crayons in bulk).
• Clean detergent boxes can be used for magazines and catalogs (stored vertically) or for construction paper and other types of paper (stored flat with open end out).
• Stacking office trays are good paper storage.
• Rather than storing lots of magazines and catalogs, cut pictures to save. Sort pictures by categories (food, animals, families, plants) and store in large mailing envelopes. Print category on outside of envelope and put in file box.
• Cake mix boxes with lids removed can store matching games, small books by subjects, or other small items. Magazine or catalog pictures can be stored in cake mix boxes. Store on a shelf with bookends (like books).
• Cardboard file boxes or copier paper boxes can be used to store larger, recyclable materials. Place lid under box for added stability and easy access.
• Store beans, pasta, rice, or similar items in 2-liter bottles. This type of storage provides good visibility and pours easily.
• Dress-up clothes can be placed on hangers and hung on clothing rods.
• A laundry basket can hold purses and shoes.

Leader Pack Items/Resource Kit Items
• Store kit books on shelves with other books in the resource room (see above).
• File teaching pictures in a general picture file (p.121).
• Sort Bible markers by reference, place in envelopes, and store in a sturdy shoe box or shallow file box.
• Set up a file in a photocopy paper box, banker's box, plastic crate, or large rectangular laundry basket. Divide items by Bible concept area, Bible-learning center/activities, or type of item (stand-up figures, matching games, recipes, newsletter, and so on.) Create a divider for each area out of cardboard or poster board cut to fit the file box or basket. Print the category at the top of the divider.
• Prepare each kit item so it will be ready for use. Cut pieces apart, cover with clear contact plastic, or assemble as needed. Store items with multiple pieces in a zip-lock bag or pocket file folder. On a self-adhesive label, print the name of the item and the category in which it belongs. Attach the label to the front of the bag or folder. Photocopy the instructions from the instruction sheet, back of kit envelope, or teaching guide. Glue the instructions on an index card and place the card inside the bag or folder. If using ziplock bags, you may want to cut a piece of cardboard or poster board to fit inside the bag to

help the bag stand in the file.
• File each item in the appropriate category.

Teaching Pictures—Set up a file in a photocopy paper box, banker's box, plastic crate, or large rectangular laundry basket. Decide how you will divide the teaching pictures. Use subject areas such as Old Testament, New Testament, Jesus, Church, Family, God, God's Creation, Self, Others, Community, World. Add subject areas as needed. Create a divider for each subject area out of cardboard or poster board cut to fit the file box or basket. Print the subject area at the top of the divider. File the pictures behind the dividers. Smaller teaching pictures can be stored in vinyl sheet protectors in a three-ring binder, using the same subject areas.

What If I Don't Have a Resource Room?
Every church needs storage space for preschool resources. Start small and expand as possible. Look around your church. Is there a forgotten closet or abandoned nook full of outdated curriculum and broken metal chairs? Clean it out and put the space to work! Be creative. Add storage cabinets to the unused end of a room. Use the end of a hallway to create a new room. Check under stairwells, behind organ chambers, and under the baptistry. Put your creativity to work and locate some space.

Yes, teaching preschoolers takes stuff. With a little creativity, a few resources, and a little work, you can have an ample supply of teaching materials. You can have what you need to create a fun and interesting learning environment for preschoolers. And you can use all those resources to guide preschoolers in their first steps toward faith and a lifetime of learning about Jesus.

A Representative List of Bible Verses and Phrases

Concepts: G=God; J=Jesus; B=Bible; C=Church; S=Self; F=Family; GC=God's Creation; CW=Community/World

Reference	Bible Verse or Phrase	Concepts	Age
Genesis 1:1	In the beginning, God created the world.	G, GC	K
Genesis 1:5	God called the light day and the darkness night.	G, GC	K
Genesis 1:11	God made the flowers.	G, GC	B–K
Genesis 1:25	God made the animals.	G, GC	B–K
Genesis. 1:27	God made people.	G, GC, S	B–K
Genesis 1:31	Everything God made was very good.	G, GC	1s–K
Genesis 2:19	God made every kind of animal and bird.	G, GC	Pre-K–K
Genesis 28:15	I am with you wherever you go.	G, S	3s–K
Exodus 3:12	God said, "I will be with you."	G, S	K
Exodus 15:1	I will sing to God.	G	K
Exodus 20:12	Obey your father and mother.	F	K
Ruth 1:16	Where you go I will go, and where you live I will live.	F	K
Ruth 2:4	May God take care of you.	G, S, CW	3s–K
1 Chronicles 16:29	Bring an offering to thank God.	C	K
1 Chronicles 17:13	God will always love me.	G, S	B–K
Nehemiah 8:10	Give to others and be happy.	CW,	B–K
Job 37:14	Think about the wonderful things God made.	G, GC	Pre-K–K
Psalm 9:2	Be glad and sing songs to God.	C, G	B–K
Psalm 46:1	God helps us.	CW, G, S	B–K
Psalm 47:6	Sing praises to God.	C	B–Pre-K
Psalm 66:19	God hears me when I talk to Him.	G, S	2s–K
Psalm 73:1	God is good to us.	G, GC	B-K
Psalm 100:3	God made us.	CW	B–K
Psalm 104:14	God makes the grass grow.	G, GC	B–K
Psalm 104:17	The birds make their nests.	G, GC	Pre-K–K
Psalm 107:1	God loves us.	G, CW, S	B–Pre-K
Psalm 107:1	Give thanks to God for He is good.	G, CW, S	Pre-K–K
Psalm 122:1	I like to go to church.	C	B–Pre-K
Psalm 122:1	I was glad when they said, "Let us go to church."	C	Pre-K; K
Psalm 136:1	Say thank you to God.	S, G	B–Pre-K
Psalm 136:25	God gives food to us.	G, GC	B-Pre-K
Psalm 139:14	I am wonderfully made.	S	3–K
Psalm 147:8	God makes the grass grow.	G, GC	B–K
Psalm 147:9	God gives food to animals.	G, GC	B–K
Psalm 147:18	God makes the wind blow.	G, GC	Pre-K-K
Proverbs 17:17	A friend loves at all times.	CW	1s–K
Proverbs 20:12	God gave us ears to hear and eyes to see.	S	3s–K
Jeremiah 1:5	God said, "Before you were born, I knew you."	CW, S	K
Jeremiah 1:8	God said, "Do not be afraid. I am with you."	CW, S	K
Jeremiah 5:24	God sends the rain.	G, GC	B-Pre-K
Jeremiah 10:13	God makes the lightning flash.	G, GC	3s–K
Jeremiah 29:11	God has plans for you.	CW, S	3s–K

Micah 4:2	God will teach us how to live.	G, C, S, CW	3s–K
Zechariah 8:16	Speak the truth to each other	CW, S, F	K
Malachi 3:10	Bring an offering to church.	C	Pre-K–K
Matthew 2:1	Jesus was born.	J	B–K
Matthew 2:11	The wise men worshiped Jesus.	J	Pre-K–K
Matthew 2:23	Jesus lived in Nazareth.	J	K
Matthew 8:20	The birds have nests.	G, GC	Pre-K–K
Matthew 16:16	Peter answered, "You are the Son of God."	J	3s–K
Matthew 28:7	Jesus is alive!	J	K
Matthew 28:20	Tell about Jesus.	CW	B–K
Mark 1:17	Jesus said, "Come, follow Me."	J, S, B	3s–K
Mark 3:14	Jesus chose helpers.	J	B–K
Mark 3:14	Jesus chose twelve disciples.	J	K
Mark 10:14	Jesus said, "Let the children come to Me."	J	3s–K
Mark 10:16	Jesus loved the children.	J	B–2s
Mark 12:30	Love God.	S, G	B–Pre-K
Mark 12:31	Love others as you love yourself.	J, S, F, CW	K
Luke 1:13	God hears your prayers.	G, S	3s–K
Luke 1:31	You will call Him Jesus.	J	3s–K
Luke 2:27	Jesus went to church with His family.	F, J, C	B–K
Luke 2:38	Thank You, God, for Jesus.	J	B–Pre-K
Luke 2:52	Jesus grew tall.	J	B–Pre-K
Luke 2:52	Jesus grew tall and became wise.	J	Pre-K–K
Luke 3:18	John told others about Jesus.	J, B	B–K
Luke 4:16	Jesus read the Bible at church.	B, J, C	B–K
Luke 4:21	Jesus said, "The Bible tells about Me."	B, J, C	3s–K
Luke 5:3	Jesus taught the people.	J	3s–K
Luke 6:27	Love other people and be kind.	CW, S,	B–K
Luke 6:31	As you want others to do for you, do the same to them.	CW, C, S	K
Luke 7:21	Jesus made sick people well.	J	B–K
Luke 10:3	Jesus said, "Go! I am sending you."	J, CW	K
Luke 10:37	Jesus said, "Go and help others.	J, CW	3s–Pre-K
Luke 11:1	Teach us to pray.	J, B, S	3s–K
Luke 22:19	Jesus said, "Remember Me."	J	B–K
Luke 24:27	Jesus taught His disciples about Himself.	J	K
John 1:3	God made all things.	G	B–Pre-K
John 1:3	All things were made by God.	G	K
John 3:16	God so loved the world that He gave His Son.	G, J, W	K
John 13:15	Jesus said, "You should do as I have done for you."	J, S, G	K
John 13:34	Love one another as I have loved you.	J, S, B, W	K
John 15:9	Jesus said, "I love you."	J, S, CW	B–K
John 15:12	Jesus loves you.	J, S, CW	B–Pre-K
John 15:14	Jesus said, "You are My friends."	J, S, CW	B–Pre-K
John 15:17	Jesus said, "Love one another."	J, S, CW	B–K
John 17:1	Jesus talked to God.	J	B–Pre-K
John 17:9	Jesus prayed for His friends.	J, CW	3s–K
John 17:9	Jesus prayed for His disciples.	J, CW	K
John 17:17	The Bible is true.	B	3s–K
John 21:16	Jesus, You know that I love You.	J, S	3s–K

Acts 5:29	We must obey God.	G, S	K
Acts 5:42	People at church told others about Jesus.	C, J, CW	3s–K
Acts 8:35	Philip told the good news about Jesus.	J, CW	3s–K
Acts 10:38	Jesus went about doing good.	J	3s–K
Acts 17:26	God made all people.	G, W	B–Pre-K
Acts 18:26	Priscilla and Aquila taught Apollos about God.	C, G	K
1 Corinthians 3:9	We work together.	CW	B–Pre-K
1 Corinthians 3:9	We work together with God.	CW	K
2 Corinthians 1:24	We are helpers.	CW	B–K
2 Corinthians 9:7	God loves a cheerful giver.	CW, C	3s–K
Galatians 5:13	Help one another.	CW	B–K
Galatians 5:13	Help one another in love.	CW	K
Ephesians 4:32	Be kind to one another.	CW, C	1s–K
Colossians 1:3	We give thanks to God.	C	Pre-K–K
1 Thessalonians 4:11	Work with your hands.	CW, S	K
1 Timothy 5:4	Take care of your family.	F, S	3s–K
1 Timothy 6:17	God gives us things to enjoy.	G, GC	Pre-K–K
2 Timothy 1:3	I thank God.	S, G	B–K
2 Timothy 3:15	The Bible teaches us about Jesus.	J, B	B–K
2 Timothy 3:16	The Bible teaches us what is true.	B	3s–K
Hebrews 13:6	God helps me. I will not be afraid.	G, S	3s–K
James 5:16	Pray for each other.	CW	3s–K
1 Peter 5:7	God cares for you.	G, S	B–K
1 John 3:22	Do those things that are pleasing to God.	G, S	K
1 John 4:9	God sent His only Son, Jesus.	G, J, CW	K

Your leader guide lists additional Bible verses and phrases to use while teaching preschoolers.

Use these 15-minutes conferences as a guide for group study of *Teaching Preschoolers: First Steps Toward Faith.* Consider using these steps during your leadership meetings over the course of several months. You may choose to study all the steps in a 2½-hour conference.

1—Taking the First Steps Toward Faith
Prepare: Make signs for the names of the Bible concept areas on colored paper. (God; Jesus; Church; Bible, Self; Family; Creations; and Community and World.)
Encounter: Attach the biblical concept area signs to the wall, one at a time, and discuss what preschoolers can begin to understand about that concept area. Show the Biblical Concept Areas Chart (pp. 12-13). Say; "This chart shows specific Bible concepts for each age group for each concept area."
Continue: Give each leader an index card. Say: "We each have a philosophy, or set of beliefs and practices, regarding teaching preschoolers. Think about your philosophy of teaching preschoolers biblical truths. Before our next meeting, jot some statements that reflect your philosophy." Stress that each leader will be the only person to see his philosophy statements. Pray together. After the meeting, contact each leader, thanking him for attending. Remind the group to bring their philosophy statements to the next meeting.

2—Understanding the Preschoolers We Teach
Prepare: Cut out two large child figures. At the top of one figure, print ***What Do Preschoolers Need?*** Gather paper and markers. Cut several lengths of yarn (6 to 8 inches long). Make signs of the approaches to learning (pp. 20-21) on sheets of colored paper.
Encounter: Guide leaders to list some needs of preschoolers on the figure. (Include the general needs listed on p. 14.) Place the blank figure, yarn, paper, and markers on the floor. Say: "Write words that describe preschoolers on the pieces of paper and connect the words to the figure with the yarn." Discuss the words as leaders write. In your discussion, include the characteristics (pp. 16-17) and ways preschoolers learn listed from Chapter 2. Ask leaders to read the approach to learning signs, one at a time. Discuss each approach to learning.
Continue: Ask leaders to review their philosophy statements. Tell them to add other statements, as necessary, in light of discussion about preschoolers. Say: "As you plan to teach this week, think about the approaches to learning. What approach does each child in your class use? Are you providing activities that meet each child's approach?"

3—Getting into Focus: Partnering with Parents
Prepare: Place a large sheet of paper on the wall for brainstorming. Print the list of "10 Ways to Ruin Relationships with Parents" (p. 28) on paper strips, one way per strip. Place the strips in a gift bag.
Encounter: Discuss that the home is the first and central place of Bible teaching. Say: "Teachers and parents must partner together for biblical teaching." Brainstorm characteristics of preschool parents. Ask, "How do these characteristics impact what we do at church?" Pass the bag to leaders, encouraging them to take a strip of paper. Ask leaders to read the statements in order, one at a time. Discuss the actions that impact relationships with parents.
Continue: Encourage leaders to contact parents of each child in their classes. After the meeting, contact each leader, making sure that she has all necessary information to contact parents

4—Teaching Preschoolers the Bible
Prepare: Make a sign for each of these three questions: *How do I prepare to teach preschoolers Bible truths? What do I do during the session to guide preschoolers toward understanding Bible truths? What do I do after the session to encourage application of Bible truths?* Make signs for these words: *Teacher Connection; Kid Connections (Bible-Learning Activities and Group Time); Family Connection.* Cut out a "7" for each leader.
Encounter: Display the three questions. Say; "These are three questions teachers often ask as they think about teaching preschoolers." Place the word *Teacher Connection* near the first question. Say: "Teachers prepare through personal Bible study and planning for teaching." Show teachers a "Teacher Connection" section of a session. Place the word *Kid Connections (Bible-Learning Activities and Group Time)* near the second

question. Direct teachers to the "Bible-Learning Activities and Groups" sections of a session. Briefly discuss the use of Bible conversation and how to connect Bible Truths during a session. Call attention to the room diagrams (pp. 36-39). Place the word *Family Connection* near the third question. Say: "Bible teaching is continued during the week by parents." Show leaders the "Family Connection" section of a session.

Continue: Give each leader a number "7." Say: "Place this number where you will see it often during the week. It represents the number of days you are a preschool teacher." After the meeting, call your leaders. Ask if they have any questions about how to help preschoolers encounter Bible truths at church. Pray with them for their ministry to preschoolers.

5—Setting the Tone

Prepare: Display a piece of paper with the question "What is discipline?" Place felt-tip markers near the question. Print the statements from *LOVE THE CHILDREN* (pp.43-45) on paper strip; one entry per strip. (Be sure to number the strips.) Place the strips around the room.

Encounter: Encourage leaders to write their answers to the question on the piece of paper. After everyone has an opportunity, read the list. Then Say: "The goal of discipline is teaching. We want to teach children to have self-discipline." Guide leaders to find the paper strips. Discuss tips for guiding behavior using the strips.

Continue: Pray together, asking God to help each leader show love for the children. Say: "This week, go to your classroom when it is empty. Sit on the floor and look around. Do you see anything that could stimulate inappropriate behavior?"

6—Teaching Bible Truths Through Art and Nature/Science

Prepare: Inside two large mailing envelopes, place a copy of *Teaching Preschoolers: First Steps Toward Faith*, paper, and a pencil. Print *Art* on the front of one envelope and *Nature/Science* on the front of the other envelope. Gather ziplock plastic bags, one per leader.

Encounter: Number the leaders, alternating between 1 and 2. Ask all 1's to gather in a group; give the group the Art envelope. Ask all 2's to form another group, and give them the Nature/Science envelope. Ask each group to turn to the appropriate chapter and discuss the values of their center. (Chapter 8 for Art and Chapter 12 for Nature and Science.) Ask the groups to list guidelines for setting up the center and tips for teachers related to using the center to teach Bible truths. After a few minutes, ask each group to report.

Continue: Give each leader a ziplock bag. Ask leaders to think of as many ways as they can for using a ziplock bag in the art center and nature/science center. Tell them you will call them before the next meeting to get their list. Before the next meeting, contact each leader for their recorded lists. Compile the lists and give a copy to each leader at the next meeting.

7—Teaching Bible Truths Through Blocks/Construction and Puzzles/Manipulatives

Prepare: Inside two large mailing envelopes, place a copy of *Teaching Preschoolers: First Steps Toward Faith*, paper, and a pencil. Print *Blocks/Construction* on one envelope and *Puzzles/Manipulatives* on the other envelope. Gather index cards (the same number as leaders). Print *Blocks* on half of the cards and *Puzzles* on the other half. Place the index cards in a bag.

Encounter: Guide the leaders to each choose a card from the bag. Ask leaders to form two groups based on their cards. Give groups the appropriate envelope. Ask each group to turn to the appropriate chapter and discuss the values of their center (Blocks–Chapter 10 and Puzzles-Chapter11.) Ask the groups to list guidelines for setting up the center and tips for teachers related to using the center to teach Bible truths. After a few minutes, ask each group to report.

Continue: Pray, thanking God for the opportunity to use play to teach preschoolers the Bible. After the meeting, print the verse **We work together** on index cards. Cut each card into several pieces to make a puzzle. Mail a puzzle to each leader.

8—Teaching Bible Truths Through Homeliving/Dramatic Play

Prepare: Tape large pieces of paper to the wall and place a marker nearby. Print the guidelines for "Cooking with Preschoolers" on paper strips, one per strip. Print these words on a piece of paper: "Look at the housewares area of a discount store, especially the kitchen gadgets section. (Or look through the drawers in your kitchen.) List three safe items that could be used with preschoolers in a homeliving/dramatic play center to teach Bible truths." Make copies of the instructions and place the copies in envelopes, one per envelope. (Make enough for each leader.)

Encounter: Discuss the values of homeliving and dramatic play with the group. On a large piece of paper, list guidelines for setting up these center. Ask: "What is a prop box and how is it used?" Discuss "Guidelines for Teachers" (see p. 69). Give leaders the paper strips with guidelines for cooking with preschoolers. Read and discuss each guideline.

Continue: Give each leader an envelope. Say: "These are your sealed orders. Bring your reports back to the next meeting."

9—Teaching Bible Truths Through Music, Books, and Pictures

Prepare: Print the values of music (p.96) on a sheet of paper, the values of books on a sheet of paper, and values of pictures (p. 100) on sheet of paper. Make a few of copies of each values list. Make three group assignment cards that read "Discuss the values. How is this type of activity used in a preschool room to teach Bible truths?" Print each of these descriptions on an index card: *1. A moving song for group time; 2. A song for the Bible verse "God loves you."; 3. A welcome song; 4. A song for children helping at church; 5. A cleanup song; 6. A song about what the children are doing (such as building with blocks)*

Encounter: Ask leaders to report on items they located for homeliving/dramatic play. Divide leaders into three groups. Give an assignment to each group. After a few minutes, allow the groups to report. Discuss how books, pictures, and music can be integrated in other centers. Discuss creating songs to familiar tunes. Divide the group into 4-6 smaller groups. Give each group a song card. The group can create a song to a familiar tune for that description. Allow the groups to sing their songs.

Continue: Gather the songs that the groups created. Type out the songs (with tune designation) and make copies. Staple sets of the songs together to create a songbook. Visit each leader before the next meeting and deliver this songbook.

10—Teaching Bible Truths During Group Time

Prepare: Print the elements of group time (pp. 103-105) on strips of paper, one per strip. Locate four different colors of paper. Cut a strip from each paper color and place the strips in the Bible at four Bible verses. (Use the list on pp. 122-124.) Tape pieces of the four colors of paper together to make a gameboard. Locate a beanbag, lined paper, and envelopes.

Encounter: Sing this song (tune "London Bridge"): "I can sing and clap my hands, clap my hands, clap my hands, I can sing and clap my hands, I am special." Allow leaders to suggest other actions and substitute those actions in the song. Display the elements of group time, one at a time. Discuss each element. Place the gameboard on the floor and allow leaders an opportunity to toss the beanbag on the board and choose the matching Bible marker. Brainstorm other ideas for Bible verse games.

Continue: Pray, asking God to lead you as you teach preschoolers about Him. Give each leader a piece of lined paper and an envelope. Say: "Write down one new idea you had about group time. Then put your paper in the envelope and address it to yourself." Take the envelopes after the meeting and mail the envelopes to leaders sometime during the year to remind of the idea they learned in the training session.a.